You are in for a deeply mo[...] [...]
have never experienced. T[...] [...]
and who that makes you. I am oversimplifying but not overrating. If you have explored God's story as introduced in Elizabeth's first book, and therefore your own story written by his Spirit in his glorious Word, you will again have an opportunity to look at all that God is and be awed, moved, and changed forever. This study is wildly inviting for individuals and groups of two or more. You will develop eyes of faith and hope to not just see your story, but to know it must be lived to the fullest as you see with your mind and heart the truths in the Word that reassure us all that God's story and ours is going somewhere! You will be entering your story with those of your group, living your stories together as you share authentically and praying them together. These times will be full of glorious thanksgiving and praise. We know the end of the story for all of us who call on the name of Jesus—the fulfillment of our hope and purpose. This is truly a study like no other.

—**Nancy Puryear,** women's ministry director, Christ Community Church, Franklin, Tennessee

What a gospel-saturated gift Elizabeth Turnage has given us in her new book, *Living God's Story of Grace*. Anchored in the text of the Scriptures, singing with the beauty of grace, Elizabeth's book helps us find our place in God's big story—the doxological drama of redemptive love and restoration that unfolds from Genesis through Revelation. Accessible to the youngest believer and helpful to the most mature, *Living God's Story of Grace* will have multiple applications: Sunday school classes, leadership training, small groups, friendship enrichment, gospel coaching, and mentoring relationships, to name several. This is story-work at its best—highlighting *God's* story yet showing us our significant place *in* that story.

—**Scotty Smith,** pastor for preaching, teaching, and worship, Christ Community Church, Franklin, Tennessee

Elizabeth Turnage understands the power of story, the power of God and Scripture, the power of prayer, and the power of shared stories in community. She puts all this together in calling readers to see God's story in their own, to share their stories with each other, and thereby to give their individual and collective stories greater richness and meaning. This is a book that will change lives.

–**Daniel Taylor**, professor of English, Bethel University, St. Paul, Minnesota

PRAISE FOR *LEARNING GOD'S STORY OF GRACE*

Elizabeth Turnage is quite a writer. Her storytelling is compelling and engaging. I've often started to read something she has written with the intention of reading a little bit each day and found myself unable to put it down until I finished. I know her writing has ministered to my soul and to many others.

–**Tremper Longman III**, Robert H. Gundry Professor of Biblical Studies, Westmont College, Santa Barbara, California

To read Elizabeth's words is to understand the relationship between the lyric and music of a great song. Her passion to tell the Big Story of redeeming love through the everyday events and often the crises of life reveals the melody of God's grace and the beauty of his truth. Some people write a book because they want to be understood. Elizabeth writes so others will dance.

–**Scotty Smith**, pastor for preaching, teaching, and worship, Christ Community Church, Franklin, Tennessee

LIVING
GOD'S
STORY OF
GRACE

LIVING STORY BOOKS

Learning God's Story of Grace
Living God's Story of Grace

LIVING GOD'S STORY OF GRACE

Elizabeth Reynolds Turnage

PUBLISHING

P.O. BOX 817 • PHILLIPSBURG • NEW JERSEY 08865-0817

Unless otherwise indicated, all Scripture quotations are from the HOLY BIBLE, NEW INTERNATIONAL VERSION®. NIV®. Copyright © 1973, 1978, 1984 by International Bible Society. Used by permission of Zondervan Publishing House. All rights reserved.

Scripture quotations marked (ESV) are from *ESV Bible* ® (*The Holy Bible, English Standard Version* ®). Copyright © 2001 by Crossway Bibles, a publishing ministry of Good News Publishers. Used by permission. All rights reserved.

ISBN: 978-1-59638-439-2 (spiral pbk)
ISBN: 978-1-59638-548-1 (ePub)
ISBN: 978-1-59638-547-4 (Mobi)

Printed in the United States of America

CONTENTS

ACKNOWLEDGMENTS

Through the small and large surrenders in minute and momentous struggles, God perfects our faith. Often he sends special companions to help us along during difficult seasons. This text has begun, continued, and ended for me with a long, hard season of three separate shoulder surgeries. Two persistent healers have walked the road of suffering with me, showing me what it means to hope and believe on another's behalf. For their unflagging persistence in bringing new health to me, I thank:

My longsuffering husband, the madly skilled orthopedic surgeon Kip Turnage.

And my brilliant, kind, and ever-humorous physical therapist, Ken Byrd.

Faith and hope grow as we tell and hear one another's stories. I would like to thank two deeply faithful and profoundly hopeful women, Heather Ferguson and Hope Parker, for so graciously telling their stories.

Kip and I are blessed to walk with four uniquely storied children of faith, now young men and women who believe and hope and love together. Robert, Mary Elizabeth, Jackie, and Kirby: in your lives, God reveals his unfailing love.

Finally, to the many companions who encourage me to set my hope anew on the Lord, your names are in my heart, and I thank our God in every remembrance of you.

INTRODUCTION

In our hometown of Pensacola, Florida, hurricane stories are a part of local lore. After one devastating hurricane, I was trading tales with a fellow soccer mom. After telling her about our action-packed evacuation, I asked her what she and her family had done. Her answer made me want to laugh—and cry: "We stayed inside and thought happy thoughts." At first it seemed ludicrous. "What earthly good did you think that would do?" I thought. But then I realized that the happy-thought approach may be the only hope for a world without a larger narrative.

The twenty-first century has ushered in the grand era of disbelief or any-belief. Believe in nothing, because there is nothing to believe in. Or believe anything you want; just don't trample on my belief. One bumper sticker expresses the attitude toward hope: "I've given up hope and I feel much better." To many struggling hearts of the twenty-first century, faith and hope are at worst scornworthy and at best silly.

The Bible tells us that Christian believers also struggle with faith and hope. "Lord, I believe; help my unbelief!" (Mark 9:24 NKJV). This honest cry of a father seeking healing for his son expresses the heartfelt plea of every Christ-follower who longs to live a life of faith and hope. We do believe. But we are afraid. Today we believe the gospel: Jesus has come to establish a new kingdom in the world, and he has begun the process of restoring

9

peace and securing hope. And tomorrow (or five minutes from now or at this very moment), we fear that this King won't really rescue us from our struggle with the enemy of light.

When we live in fear rather than faithfulness, when heart-ache overcomes hopefulness, we often try to take matters into our own hands to bring certain endings to small stories. Remembering the redemption stories that Scripture tells as well as the ones that God has written into our lives helps us to surrender trust back to its rightful object: our Savior King. It is in God's faithfulness, not our own, that we trust (faith) and wait (hope).

Living lives of the radical faith and extremist hope to which the gospel calls us is the best way to communicate God's story of grace to a bewildered and searching world that looks into its own heart and sees nobody home. God gives us faith and hope; he deepens these qualities as we live them out in daily life. In part 1 of the Living Story series, we learned the central narrative of Christian believers; in part 2, we will explore what it means to live this story in faith and hope.

God's Story of Grace and Faith and Hope

To begin understanding how these core themes of our lives function, let's review what we studied in *Learning God's Story of Grace*.

- **Creation:** God creates the cosmos with order and purpose. He creates humans in his image, with dignity and for delight, with differentiation and for dominion. In this beginning chapter of redemptive history, humans live in a state of shalom, a state of "rest." Faith and hope characterize their lives.
- **Fall:** Adam and Eve, succumbing to Satan's suggestion, decide that they know better than God what they need

for life and beauty. In a dramatic act of faithlessness, they consciously rebel against God's command not to eat of the tree of the knowledge of good and evil. Unwilling to wait (hope), they take and eat, and immediately they experience shame and alienation. They turn to hiding, blaming, and shaming (putting their hope in something other than God) in futile attempts to restore lost shalom.

- **Redemption:** God, the faithful pursuer of his lost children, offers an immediate reason for hope, announcing the plan for redemption, telling a story of a coming chapter when Eve's offspring (Christ) will crush Satan. The remainder of Scripture continues the story of the perfectly faithful Savior, Jesus Christ. In him alone we experience promised rest.

- **Consummation:** Hope is focused on the resurrection of Christ and the "one day" when he will come again, bringing with him God's New Jerusalem. The momentum of the story toward the complete restoration of shalom provides the foundation for a life of faith and hope now.

LIVING THE STORY

Scripture calls us to learn and rehearse God's story of grace, because doing so calls us to live a life of faith, hope, and love—the essence of worship:

- Faith means trusting in God for life and hope rather than other gods.
- Hope means believing that God is doing brand-new things in the midst of wrecked shalom.
- Love is living in and telling our story to a broken world sorely in need of a life-transforming story.

11

THE GUIDE

This Bible study aims to bring the transforming power of the gospel to bear on your life. As you interact with this material, I hope you will experience the freedom to live in God's story of grace with deeper faith, greater hope, and more passionate love. The format is designed to take you into the grand narrative of Scripture, your story, and others' stories by giving you opportunities to pray about and live what you are studying. The following sections will help you go deeper:

Engaging Scripture. Here you will focus on a passage or story from Scripture and answer questions for insight, reflection, and discussion. This draws us to worship God and follow Christ.

Theological Theme. This section discusses a theme that God consistently reveals through Scripture.

Entering Your Story. This section takes the passage and shifts the focus to what God is writing in your story. Here you will be given opportunities to write and tell your story.

Living Story. This section invites you to reflect on how you will live out the gospel in the topic being explored.

Praying Story. The final section offers an opportunity to write or say prayers regarding the story.

Here are a few suggestions to help you get the most out of the Bible study:

Just do it! As a former stoic, I used to embrace this Nike slogan, but it didn't always lead to love. While I don't want you to fall into the trap of doing duty, I do want you to engage the material. If the only thing you can do is to read the Scripture, make sure you do that. The Bible is the living Word of God. Unlike any self-help book, just reading it transforms you! But please, do more.

Interact with the questions. The studies are divided into suggested amounts of material to cover over a five-day period. This gives you two extra days! Use the space in the book, or if you need more room, get a journal or create a document on your computer for walking through this guide. Let the questions wander around in your brain as you commute to work or clean the kitchen, and then write some things down. You may think you don't need to write anything down, but trust me (or at least trust cognition theorists)—we learn, understand, and grow as we write.

Pray. Ask the Holy Spirit, whom God has given as "the Helper" to come alongside you (John 14:26), to be your primary guide in the process of learning and living story. Specific exercises for prayer are provided in each chapter.

Tell and listen. Each individual reflects God's story of grace in a unique way. Gift others by sharing your responses and your story. If you tend to be more talkative, make room for the quieter ones to speak. Always listen carefully to others.

Enjoy. We were made to worship, to give and receive delight in God's story of grace. My deepest hope is that you will enjoy being transformed by the gospel, the amazing true story in which we are called to live and love.

May God richly bless us all as we learn the narrative of life and love in Jesus Christ, which God is telling everywhere, all the time!

1

FAITH AND HOPE DEFINED

Surrendering in Trust and Seeing the Unseen

KEY THEMES

- God generously gifts us with faith and hope.

- Faith and hope rest on unseen spiritual realities, not present earthly realities.

- Faith and hope are nurtured and flourish in community.

DAY 1

Screeching—the word that best describes the timbre of my voice. A far cry from the soft tone of a woman presumably calmed by faith, encouraged by hope. My husband winced at the punctuation of each of my loud exclamations (though I notice this only in the mental replay of the ugly scene). Finally, my anger fizzled like the last gasp of air leaving a balloon: "I've lost all hope that this shoulder will ever get better." Tears welled. "I will *always* live in this pain."

This scene occurred near the end of the eighth month of my recovery from rotator cuff surgery, a day when pain and frustration eroded almost all semblance of gospel sanity. It felt perversely good to give up on hope; it also felt horrible.

Thankfully, two primary characters in the story had not given up hope. My husband (an orthopedic surgeon) and my physical therapist faithed me and hoped me. It was as if they could see inside my shoulder and describe the unseen to me. Because of past cases similar to mine, they could believe for me that relief would come with a little more time and continued strengthening. They believed the reality that is the essence of hope: "This will make a really good story one day."

Though this unsightly kitchen-table drama centers on earthly hope—that my pain would subside in this life—it reveals some important realities about spiritual faith and hope:

- Faith and hope are gifts from God that rely not on our goodness but on his rich mercy and grace.
- Faith and hope rest not on circumstances in this life but on unseen and certain spiritual realities about the story of grace that God has written and is writing.
- Faith and hope are lived in community. God uses his Word and other people to remind us of past rescue and to direct us toward our future hope—the day when true shalom will be restored forever and ever.

Living between the two comings of Christ, Christians are to look backward and forward: back to the manger, the cross, and the empty tomb, whereby salvation was won for them; forward to their meeting with Christ beyond this world, their personal resurrection, and the joy of being with their Savior in glory forever.

—J. I. Packer, *Concise Theology*

In this chapter, we explore the themes of faith and hope through several Scriptures and stories. Join me as we step into the varying terrain of unseen reality.

ENGAGING SCRIPTURE: HEBREWS; 1 PETER; ROMANS; 2 CORINTHIANS

Background

Genre. Epistle. Epistles are letters written to early Christians to help them live the Christian story in context of their current circumstances.

Context. Hebrews: Hebrews differs from other epistles because it is written in the form of a sermon. The author (uncertain; Paul, Clement, Luke, and Apollos have been suggested) writes to Jewish Christians enduring trials. He encourages them to cling to their faith because their faith is in Jesus Christ, the superior Priest who is their Savior.

1 Peter: The apostle Peter writes to suffering Christians to encourage them to persevere in faith and hope because God is rescuing and redeeming now and for eternity.

Romans: The apostle Paul writes to the Romans to teach them about God's gift of righteousness in Christ.

2 Corinthians: The apostle Paul writes to the Corinthians, defending his life and ministry. Some opponents had argued that Paul's suffering meant that he couldn't be a Spirit-filled apostle of Christ. Paul responds that God uses suffering to reveal his glory and power.

1. Faith and hope are central themes in these epistles that focus on trials and suffering. Why do you think this is the case? How do trials affect your faith and hope?

What Are Faith and Hope?

2. John Calvin says, "True faith always goes hand in hand with hope." Read the following verses and describe the relationship between faith and hope.

   a. 1 Peter 1:21

   b. Hebrews 6:11–12

   c. 1 Thessalonians 1:3

Faith in Jesus Christ is what saves us. Hope sustains perseverance in faith. One definition of faith and hope can be found in Hebrews 11:1–3.

3. Read Hebrews 11:1. Two balanced parts tell us what faith is.

   a. Look up Hebrews 11:1 in the New International Version (NIV) and the English Standard Version (ESV). (If necessary, you can find different translations at www.biblegateway.com to do this.) Fill in the blanks with the words that complete each part.

   NIV:

   Faith is _____ of _____ and _____ of _____.

   ESV:

   Faith is the _____ of _____, the _____ of _____.

   b. It seems paradoxical (opposite of what seems true) to say that faith is certainty of something that we haven't seen yet. How would you answer someone who pointed out this paradox?

The Spirit of God shows us hidden things, the knowledge of which cannot reach our senses. . . . We are told of the resurrection of the blessed, but meantime we are involved in corruption; we are declared to be just, and sin dwells within us; we hear that we are blessed, but meantime we are overwhelmed by untold miseries; we are promised an abundance of good things, but we are often hungry and thirsty; God proclaims that He will come to us immediately, but seems to be deaf to our cries. What would happen to us if we did not rely on our hope, and if our minds did not emerge above the world out of the midst of darkness through the shining Word of God and by His Spirit? Faith is rightly called the substance of things which are still the objects of hope and the evidence of things not seen.

—John Calvin, *Hebrews*

4. Read Hebrews 11:3.

   a. What does faith help us to understand and see?

   b. Why is this important?

⚙ Choose a verse to memorize. Write it here and tell why you chose it.

WHERE AND WHEN DO FAITH
AND HOPE OPERATE

From Hebrews 11:1–3, we learn that faith happens when things are hoped for but not yet possessed. Faith is indefinable without hope, its future component. Let's look at the time and space in which faith and hope do their work.

1. Read Romans 15:4.

   a. What does it tell us about the purpose of Scripture?

   b. Tell of a time when you received encouragement and the ability to endure from something "written in the past."

As we learned in *Learning God's Story of Grace*, we live in the era between Christ's redemption of the cosmos through his life, death, and resurrection (the "already") and the day when Christ will return to complete the work begun (the "not yet").

WHAT RESULTS DO FAITH AND HOPE BRING?

2. In 2 Corinthians 4, we find several instructive verses about faith and hope.

   a. 4:6: What knowledge does faith give us?

   b. 4:13–15: What do we believe and speak as a result of faith, and why?

   c. 4:16–17: You may have heard the expression, "When you see a *therefore* in Scripture, you should always look at the preceding verses to see what it's 'there' 'for.'"

Consider 4:6–15. What essential truths give us reason for not losing heart and for continuing to hope?

d. 4:18: How do we live the life of faith and hope?

⚙ Review your memory verse by posting it on social media or writing it in a note or an e-mail.

In 2 Corinthians 4, Paul demonstrates that faith focuses on the finished work of Christ and that hope focuses on the future return of Christ to sustain us in present sufferings. Now let's see what faith and hope lived look like.

True faith is not only a knowledge and conviction that everything God reveals in His word is true; it is also a deep-rooted assurance, created in me by the Holy Spirit through the gospel that, out of sheer grace earned for us by Christ, not only for others, but I too, have had my sins forgiven, have been made forever right with God, and have been granted salvation. (Heidelberg Catechism, Question 21)

—Kevin DeYoung, *The Good News We Almost Forgot*

DAY 3

WHAT DO FAITH AND HOPE LOOK LIKE?

After the introductory definition of faith and hope in Hebrews 11, the author presents a list of Old Testament characters, real people, who lived it. In *The Message* paraphrase, each new character is introduced by the phrase "By an act of faith . . ." in order to emphasize that faith and hope must be lived to be real. We'll look at two examples here and enter into Abraham and Sarah's story more deeply in the coming chapters.

1. Read Hebrews 11:4-5.

   a. Why was Abel's sacrifice better than Cain's? What commendation did his faith "earn" him?

   b. What do these verses tell you about a person living a life of faith?

c. Think about it. Would you prefer that God have a system of rewards based on works? In what way might that system be easier than the free gift of forgiveness?

2. Read Hebrews 11:7.

a. What does Noah's life tell us about faithful living?

b. What acts of faith have you done that may have seemed foolish in the eyes of those who cannot see the unseen?

WHERE DO THEY ORIGINATE?

3. Read Hebrews 6:13-14. What does it teach about the origins of faith?

DAY 4

ENTERING YOUR STORY

We've seen what Scripture says about faith and hope; we've explored the stories of several Old Testament characters to see it lived. Let's now study God's story of grace in our lives to sharpen our eyesight for the unseen. Listen to one woman's story of faith, hope, and community:

My friend Heather, a missionary in Peru, was struggling with homesickness and weariness. She and her husband thought a trip back to Texas would offer just the renewed vision and energy she needed. Less than two weeks before her planned departure, she received heartbreaking news: the eighteen-month-old son of their former associate pastor and wife had nearly drowned:

"For the next ten days we were given daily updates by phone regarding Knox's condition. We prayed and prayed that God would give Knox back life. The tenth day after the accident, Knox died.

"God had just put our friends on the most difficult path I could ever imagine. Losing a child, to me, was the hardest thing, the worst thing, that anybody would ever experience."

Heather made her trip home, but the focus of her trip had changed—she would go to support and encourage her friends:

"The service was awful and amazing. Who ever wants to be at a child's funeral? But our pastors, including Knox's father, spoke truth and comfort boldly, honestly, and with a rawness that could come only from the brokenness of grief. I left stunned and devastated."

Theological Theme: Regeneration

Regeneration comes from two Latin roots: *re-*, meaning "again," and *gen-*, meaning "create." In *Learning God's Story of Grace*, we learned about how shalom (the peace, harmony, and dignity with which God created the world) was spoiled by the fall. The image of God in humankind was disfigured and distorted in such a way that we no longer fully reflect the glory of God as we once did.

Those who have faith have experienced regeneration, being "born again." In John 3:1–5, the knowledgeable religious leader Nicodemus earnestly questions Jesus about this new way of life he teaches. Jesus teaches him that this radical kingdom-life is for those who are "born again." The Spirit, he says, gives birth to new life. Nicodemus is understandably confused about the process.

Nicodemus, like us, must understand that because we are dead in sin, we need a new heart in order to repent of (turn away from) our sin and believe in God. The Holy Spirit generates this new heart and, with it, gives us the power to believe. Thankfully, our faith and hope come from the One who has the power to sustain it—if it were up to us, we would flounder.

God regenerates hearts in order that we might live holy lives and love the broken world. With the newborn eyes of faith and hope, we envision redemption in the most shattered of places, laboring in the Spirit's power to re-create beauty and draw others to know the Savior. (Related verse: 2 Cor. 3:18. See also Eph. 4:23; Col. 3:10.)

Heather writes about the community's struggle in the days following the funeral:

"The feelings of grief, guilt, brokenness, doubt all hovered around the hearts and minds of the congregation. Faith was shaken—how could God allow this? The usual comfort of 'God will use this for good' seemed hollow in the aftermath of such tragedy. We didn't want God to use it for good—we wanted it to not have happened at all. I was heavy with the weight of a churchload of grief."

Several days after the funeral, Heather was invited to visit Knox's mother.

"What she said to me that day was the beginning of a complete paradigm shift in how I viewed suffering and faith.

"'You know, I'm not the first mother to lose a child and I won't be the last. A hundred years ago, this happened all the time. This could happen to anyone. People ask me if I'm mad at God, and yes, I am. But where else can I go—to whom else can I turn? There isn't anywhere else.'

"I was astounded by my friend's faith—the faith of the Psalm 88 writer who ended his lament with 'darkness is my closest friend.' The faith that knows words of life given in Scripture invite wrestling. The faith that knows God may ask anybody to walk the hardest path. But God! The faith that knows there is nowhere else to turn but to the sovereign God who took their precious son. The faith that believes the Father knows the depth of their heartache."

Heather's story and Knox's mother's story are ones of rich faith and deep hope. Suffering is not eliminated. Surrender comes only through wrestling.

Now it's your turn to reflect on God's work of faith and hope in your life. Choose one of the following topics to reflect on your story.

Where can I go from your Spirit? Where can I flee from your presence?

—Psalm 139:7

1. Some people recall a precise time of being "born from above"; for others, it was a gradual experience that happened over time or happened when they were very young.

   a. Do you remember when you "came to faith," you suddenly believed, you were "born again," or something about your belief was secured in a new way? Tell that story.

b. What new understanding did you have? What changes did you desire to make in your life? How did you see the Holy Spirit operating?

2. Have you ever had an experience like Heather's—of faith and hope growing as a result of a tragedy? Tell that story.

a. What happened to challenge your faith and hope?

b. What new revelations about God's character did you gain?

❁ Review your memory verse.

DAY 5

LIVING STORY

1. "The only thing that counts is faith expressing itself through love" (Gal. 5:6). As we have seen, faith and hope do not exist in the abstract; only lived do they become reality.

   a. As a group or as individuals, pray about an act of service that you might want to do together as an expression of faith and hope. It might be something that you've been afraid to risk or have never imagined yourself doing. It might be a service performed by one of your group members that others would like to try. (Examples: serving in soup kitchens or on the streets; buying a meal for a homeless person and sitting with her while she eats it . . .)

b. Choose a time to do this act of faith as a group or as individuals.

PRAYING STORY

Triune God, Father, Son, and Holy Spirit, we bow before you, so very grateful that you regenerated our stilled and spoiled hearts. Knowing that we are impotent to re-create ourselves, you poured your Spirit into us and birthed us again to bring glory to you. You know our hearts of unbelief; we entreat you to grow faith and hope in us. When we look at shattered shalom and see only earthly escape routes that result in dead-ends, enlarge our vision with your heavenly eyesight. When shaken, we cling to frail idols that appear strong; draw us again to cleave to you, who have never let us go. By you and through you and to you be all the glory, forever and ever. Amen.

Moving Forward

Living faith and hope might be compared to viewing a mountain from a distance, and then hiking along a trail leading to its summit. Along the way, we struggle at steep ascents, but we will also step easily along smooth segments. God has placed in our hearts the assurance that Christ came to renew our sinful hearts and to restore broken shalom; he has given us clear views of the certain consummation at Christ's return. As we study the stories of real people in Scripture and our own lives, we learn some of the contours of faith and hope. Let's continue by looking at Abraham's story and the call of faith to let go and look forward.

2

ABRAHAM'S STORY

Letting Go and Looking Forward

KEY THEMES

- ❁ Faith involves a transfer of trust from the seen and temporal to the unseen and eternal.

- ❁ God calls us by faith to leave "home" and follow him.

- ❁ God gives faith by grace and justifies us by faith.

DAY 1

About two hours into a five-hour flight from Atlanta to Seattle, I ventured into conversation with my seat partner, a distinguished-looking middle-aged businessman. We quickly established the basics—he was a dentist from Peachtree City; I was a mom from Pensacola. He was traveling to see his daughter and her fiancé; I was on my twelfth journey to the Northwest to complete a graduate degree in Christian studies. Yes, he looked astonished when I told him what I was doing. But he didn't look at me as if I

33

had descended from Mars. Oddly, unlike almost everyone else to whom I had tried to explain the venture, he seemed to understand.

"When you tell people, do they say you're crazy?" he asked.

I shook my head. "They don't usually *say* I'm crazy. But the look in their eyes says it all."

He nodded. "Everyone thought I was crazy when I decided to go to med school when I was thirty-four." My new friend told me his story: he had left an established career as a manager in a retail chain to revisit a dream left behind, of becoming a dentist. He explained that he felt an urgency to try it, to see if he could do it. Then he asked me more about my story.

"I admire you for taking the risk," he said. "What led you to do it?"

"The only way I know to put it is—I feel *called*." He seemed to get that, so I finished the thought with a shrug: "I know I'm a fool. I just hope I'm a fool for Christ."

In the catalogue of faithful living in Hebrews and throughout the rest of the Bible, we read of people building, offering, leaving, and dying "by faith." As we noted in chapter 1, to live in faith and hope means to act, sometimes in ways that seem terribly foolish to people playing out a small storyline written by the world's norms. Faith has two crucial components:

- Leaving by letting go of the seen and seemingly certain.
- Looking forward and clinging to a promise whose certainty lies in the character of the redeeming God.

In this chapter, we will follow Abraham, who hears the call of God to leave home, family, country, and name in order to move into a new story of grace promised by God.

We profess to be strangers and pilgrims, seeking after a country of our own, yet we settle down in the most un-stranger-like fashion, exactly as if we were quite at home and meant to stay as long as we could.

—Amy Carmichael, *God's Missionary*

ᴇNGAGING ꜱCRIPTURE: ʜEBREWS; ꞡENESIS

Background

Genre. (For Hebrews, see chapter 1.) History. The title *Genesis*, a Greek word meaning "origin, source, race, or creation," signifies the purpose of Genesis: to tell the history of the beginning of God's people.

Context. Genesis 12–50 begins a portion called the "patriarchal history." *Patriarch* refers to each of the fathers of God's chosen people: Abraham, Isaac, and Jacob. Through Abraham, God will bring forth a nation that will be blessed and will be a blessing to the entire world.

Note: Abraham's name changes during the course of the story from *Abram* to *Abraham*, and Sarai's name changes to *Sarah*. Do not be confused. They are the same people. We will call them *Abraham* and *Sarah* throughout this chapter.

To understand what the letting go and looking forward of faith and hope look like, we'll follow Abraham through three significant events on his journey of faith:

- Chapter 1: Abraham's Call: Leaving his self-designed shalom as he looks forward to God's promised rest.
- Chapter 2: Faith Floundering: Failing in faith and hoping in his own solutions.
- Chapter 3: The Ultimate Test: Surrendering his most precious possession while trusting God to provide.

  1. Challenge: We will be examining portions of Abraham's story. If you're up for a challenge, try reading Genesis 12–22, the *whole* story. If you can, do it in one sitting (it will probably take about thirty to forty-five minutes).

2. Let's begin by looking at what Hebrews tells us about Abraham's faith. Read Hebrews 11:8–10. We'll use the 5 W/1 H-question approach to walk through this passage:

a. Who called Abraham (vv. 8, 10)?

b. What verbs describe what Abraham did by faith (vv. 8–10)?

c. When did he do these things (v. 8)?

d. Where did he go (v. 8)?

To the Lord each one should cry, "Lord, what wilt thou have me to do?" We, who are his chosen, redeemed from among men, called out from the rest of mankind, ought to feel that if no other ears hear the divine call, our ears must hear it; and if no other heart obeys, our soul rejoices to do so.

—Charles H. Spurgeon, "The Obedience of Faith"

e. Why did he do it (v. 10)?

f. How did Abraham do it (vv. 8–9)?

Acts 7:1–8 gives a little more background to Abraham's call, telling us that it came first in Ur. Terah leaves Ur with his family and heads toward Canaan, but stops in Haran. God comes to Abraham in Haran and calls him to finish the journey. This bit of history reveals that the call of God comes more than once and unfolds over time.

CHAPTER 1: ABRAHAM'S CALL

1. Read Genesis 12:1-3.

   a. What three things does God require Abraham to leave? What do these things represent?

   b. What things have you left behind, or do you need to leave behind, as part of living "by faith"? How has leaving these things impacted your relationship with God?

2. Underline all the times the phrase *I will* is used in verses 1–3.

   a. What does God promise Abraham?

   b. How will Abraham become a blessing to all the families of the earth? Read Galatians 3:8–9.

   c. What blessings do Christians receive through another promised Son, Jesus Christ?

We have seen that the word "blessing" is a very strong word, entailing God's *shalom*, the well-being and peace of God's kingdom. This promise indicates that God's purpose in a) making Abram a personal friend, and b) making Abram's offspring into a new human community is all for the ultimate aim of c) bringing salvation to the whole world.

—Tim Keller, *Genesis*

❁ Choose a verse to memorize from Genesis 12-22. Write the verse here and tell why you chose it.

DAY 2

CHAPTER 2: FAITH FLOUNDERING

As Abraham responds to God's call and moves toward the promise, he oscillates between faith and fear. At times, he rests in shalom, trusting in God's promise and waiting for the unseen to become a reality. At other times, he wrestles with fear and hopelessness, forgetting God's previous rescue and promised future and turning to his own schemes to bring a sense of belonging and safety. Here are some highlights of Abraham's story:

Genesis 12:10-20

Hungry and anxious to provide, Abraham heads to Egypt, where out of fear he tells Pharaoh that Sarah is his sister. God rescues Sarah, and the plan for the promised son is left intact.

Genesis 13

Abraham rests in God's promise as he allows Lot to choose his portion of the land. God reasserts his promise.

Genesis 14

Again, Abraham reveals a heart willing to let go of worldly attachments. He receives a blessing from Melchizedek, the king of Salem, and he refuses a political offer of riches from other kings.

Genesis 15

Abraham struggles with fear and doubt—*how* will he become the father of a nation, given his and Sarah's advancing years? God elevates the promise to the level of a covenant, an unbreakable treaty utterly dependent on the initiator to fulfill. From this chapter comes a crucial statement about faith: "Abraham believed the Lord, and he credited it to him as righteousness" (Gen. 15:6; Rom. 4:3).

Genesis 16

From the heights of renewed hope, Abraham tumbles into an ugly scene of surrendering to his wife's disbelief, disrupting shalom in his marriage, family, and future nation.

Genesis 17

God renews his covenantal agreement, again taking it to a new level. He changes Abram's name to *Abraham* (from "father" to "father of many nations") and Sarai's to *Sarah* (both names have the same meaning; the second seems to particularize Sarah).

Genesis 18

God visits Abraham and repeats his promise of a son in Sarah's hearing. Abraham, as a "friend" of God, believes that God can and will rescue any righteous people from Sodom and Gomorrah.

Genesis 19

Abraham watches as God fulfills his promise to save Lot and his family from the destruction of two cities characterized by worldly arrogance and widespread evil. Lot and his family look backward, clinging to the seen, revealing by contrast Abraham's growing faith eyesight.

Here we resume our deeper exploration of Abraham's story as we take an up-close look at another scene of his faithlessness.

Genesis 20

On the grounds that a man doesn't repeat such a spectacular failure, some scholars believe that the story recorded in Genesis 20 is a repeat of the story from Genesis 12:10–20. Reading the Bible, my own life, and others' lives, I think this conclusion utterly misses the point: we are prone to wander, and our sinful flesh drives us to repeat the insane moments of our lives. This story carries both a serious warning and a hopeful reality about the life of faith—it is utterly up to God, not us, to fulfill the promise.

1. Read Genesis 20:1–7.

   a. Why does Abimelech take Sarah into his harem (vv. 1–2)?

b. Who rescues Sarah from Abimelech, and how (vv. 3-7)?

c. What irony do you see in the conversation between God and Abimelech about Sarah?

2. Read Genesis 20:8-13.

a. What do you notice about the questions that Abimelech asks Abraham (vv. 8-10)?

b. Some critical scholars have suggested that Abraham's action is worse here than in chapter 12. What do you think?

   c. Can you remember times when you protected yourself through small deception? What were those times like?

3. Read Genesis 20:14–18.

   a. How is shalom restored in this story?

   b. What does this story reveal about faith and hope?

God himself, a Spirit, real but invisible, calls us to live the Adventure guided by a hand and an arm that we cannot see or prove in irrefutable terms. And this is the dwelling of faith in which we all must learn to be at home.

—Luci Shaw, *The Crime of Living Cautiously*

❂ Review your memory verse by posting it on social media or writing it in a note or an e-mail.

DAY 3

CHAPTER 3: THE ULTIMATE TEST

In a romantic comedy, Abraham and Sarah's story would end in chapter 21, with the birth of the promised child through Sarah. But the Author God has more faith to write into Abraham's story, so the ending circles back to the beginning. God has another important call for Abraham.

Note on context: The only kind of offering mentioned in Genesis calls for an animal to be burned on the altar. This offering represented the need for a sacrifice for sinful humankind to have relationship with a holy God.

1. Read Genesis 22:1–2.

   a. What does God ask Abraham to do?

   b. What similarities does this call have to God's call in Genesis 12?

c. In light of Genesis 12, why is this call so puzzling?

2. Genesis 22:3-8 describes Abraham's quick response to the call. If we read carefully, we see hints of Abraham's faith that empower him to follow this incomprehensible summons of God.

a. Notice Abraham's words to his servants (v. 5). What do they suggest about Abraham's faith?

b. What does Abraham's response to Isaac reveal about his belief (vv. 7–8)? How has Abraham learned this crucial reality in his life?

3. Read Hebrews 11:17–19. What does the narrator of Hebrews reveal about why and how Abraham was able to obey God's call?

4. Read Genesis 22:9–14.

   a. How does God provide a way for the promised son to be saved?

   b. Why do you think God waits until this exact moment to stop Abraham?

From Abraham the harrowing demand evokes only love and faith, certain as he is that the "foolishness of God" is unexplored wisdom. So he is enabled, in the surrender of his son, to mirror God's still greater love, while his faith gives him a first glimpse of resurrection. The test, instead of breaking him, brings him to the summit of his lifelong walk with God.

—Derek Kidner, *Genesis*

5. Read Genesis 22:15-18.

a. Why are these words a perfect ending to this story?

b. What do they teach us about a life of faith and hope?

Theological Theme: Justification by Faith

Abraham believed God, and it was credited to him as righteousness.

—Romans 4:3

In the first chapter of the study, we asked the question, "What does faith *do*?" One of the most important effects of faith is justification. In general language, to *justify* is to "provide reason for" or "defend." In theology, *justification by faith* means that we are declared right by the holy God on the basis of our faith in Christ.

As sinners, which we all are (Rom. 3:23), we have no justification for our sin. In the court of God's holy law, we are declared guilty. That is why Genesis 15:6 is such a radical statement. Abraham is declared "righteous," that is, "not guilty," because he believed. Abraham's righteousness does not come from his moral rectitude or good actions—it comes from his faith, which comes from God.

Faith in Christ brings an even more astounding reality to our stories. We receive the credited righteousness (see *imputed righteousness* on page 86 of *Learning God's Story*) by transferring trust from our own efforts at being good to Christ's finished work on the cross (Rom. 3:23–26). When someone confesses, "I believe Christ has fully paid the price I owe for my sin," that person is credited with Christ's righteousness (Rom. 4:23–24).

The radical concept of justification by faith should humble and astonish us. Robert Lowry, in his great old hymn, asks, "How can we keep from singing?" Indeed, when we understand that the holy God sent his holy Son as the only adequate substitute for our sins, how can we keep from living a life of loving God and loving others?

We can put it this way: the man who has faith is the man who is no longer looking at himself, and no longer looking to himself. . . . Faith makes a man say, "Yes, I have sinned grievously, I have lived a life of sin . . . yet I know that I am a child of God because I am not resting on any righteousness of my own; my righteousness is in Jesus Christ, and God has put that to my account."

—D. M. Lloyd-Jones, quoted in Keller, *Genesis*

DAY 4

ENTERING YOUR STORY

One of the many joys of studying Scripture is seeing connections between the lives of biblical characters and our own lives. When we recognize these connections, we can better understand who God is and how to worship him in our own lives. Here is my "Abraham" story, of a time when I wrestled with God over a possession that I wanted to keep as *mine*:

Background: Six months pregnant, I had flown from Atlanta to Colorado with my mom for my grandfather's funeral. Less than twelve hours after arriving, I learned that our eighteen-month-old son had been admitted to the hospital.

Less than twenty-four hours after arriving in Colorado, I was on my way back cross-country in a single-minded quest to reach our suddenly seriously ill son. This day was mostly a blur of exhaustion, silent tears, and a throbbing numbness. I stared at the seat back in front of me on the 757 jammed with jovial holiday travelers, with one determined commitment—not to break down on that plane. A nice fifty-something couple next to me asked, "When's your baby due?" And then, "Is this your first?" I wanted to scream, "NO, IT'S NOT MY FIRST! MY FIRST IS LYING FRAIL IN SOME HOSPITAL BED RIGHT THIS MINUTE WITHOUT HIS MAMA!" Somehow I managed to hold it together to explain that my grandfather had died two days before, that I had flown out for the funeral, that I was now returning to tend to our sick son. It sounded almost logical as I calmly recited it aloud.

At the hospital, the sight of our son sobered me. Our formerly live-wire child, who from birth had not known the meaning of the word *still*, now lay limp and yellow in the hospital crib. Dressed in a sickly green hospital gown, sprawled in the oversized crib with the huge metallic bars, his arm fettered by the pale plastic tubing to the IV machine beside him, he appeared to be an inmate in a bizarre infant prison. Our son was septic. "That means he has poison in his blood," the nurse explained. The plan was to give him IV antibiotics to try to kill the bacteria in his blood.

For the next four days, I waited and watched hopefully to see signs of vitality returning to my wild child. God sustained me in ways beyond imagining. I should have been exhausted—six months pregnant, flying cross-country twice in twenty-four hours, semi-sleeping in a hospital chair for three nights. How could I possibly explain the supernatural energy, the stilling comfort, or the enduring hope I experienced without the ministration of the Holy Spirit?

During the struggle, my heart rested in God's goodness. But when the agonizing days of waiting ended and our eldest son regained full health, I entered a Jacobean wrestling match with God. I could not shake the image of Abraham placing Isaac on the altar. I complained to God, "I'm not Abraham—I'm not ready to give up my only son." And God so clearly, kindly, and firmly responded, "He's not your son. He's my son."

This story stands as a living stone, a marker of the grace of God. Here I was with one young child and one in the womb. I needed to understand at the beginning of their stories this essential reality: God has gifted us with these children for a season, but they belong to *him*, and he loves them even more than we do. So much for being in "control" of my life.

1. Choose one of the following topics to reflect on your story.

   a. Calling to foolishness: When have you been called to leave something behind? Did that calling appear strange to others? What did you have to leave?

What promise did you look forward to? Why did you do it?

b. Review Hebrews 11:17–19. Have you ever been asked or forced to give up something precious to you? What sense of hope did that possession give you? What helped you to let go? What did you discover through the loss or surrendering of that possession?

⚙ Review your memory verse.

LIVING STORY

1. Begin to pray about things in your life that you believe you need or deserve in order to live. Consider relationships, work, possessions, activities. Pray specifically and journal about the following questions:

   a. What sense of security, significance, or control do these things bring?

   b. What might it look like to transfer trust from these items to God?

c. What specific, practical steps might you take to do that?

d. Write an action you could take, "by faith," and a date by which you will do it.

PRAYING STORY

2. Pray with others about the transfer of trust.

a. Write down the names of one to three people you will ask to pray with you and for you about this movement.

b. Make a date to get together with one of those people.

c. In your group, pray generally or specifically for one another to let go of idols that provide a temporary sense of significance and security.

Moving Forward

Though this chapter was named after Abraham, the "father of faith," it is clear that the hero of this story and the true Father of faith is God. God calls Abraham; God graces him with the faith to respond in obedience; God rescues Abraham; God renews the promise when Abraham falters. God has a plan—to restore his broken world—and he chooses Abraham because of his own faithfulness, not Abraham's. Because of God's steadfast love and unwavering grace, Abraham is able to let go of things that give him a temporary sense of security, significance, and hope. "By faith," Abraham moves into the unseen yet assured future of God's promised blessing. Abraham's story emphasizes that God is the initiator and sustainer of faith and hope. We will now celebrate a story feast to remember how God has conceived and nurtured our faith.

3

STORY FEASTING

An Interlude

KEY THEMES

- ✸ We are all called to tell the stories of God's "abundant goodness" (Ps. 145).

- ✸ Sharing our stories is essential to growing in faith, hope, and love because it helps us to remember redemption and to focus on future hope.

DAY 1

If you've studied part 1 in the Living Story series, you have already partaken of two story feasts. Here we reintroduce the topic for those who are new to the concept, but you veterans will find some fresh stories and thoughts here, so read on.

One of the story topics that I've feasted on frequently is the "Death of a Dream." My community's response to one painful moment reminded me of God's calling and encouraged me to persevere in trials:

"As most of you know, this summer I took a seminary class that caused me to question my foolish dream of finishing my degree. I was well on my way to reaching this impossible dream, having already completed one-third of the coursework. Each course had changed my heart profoundly and stirred a new passion for God, his calling to me, and my community. But this class was different. The professor seemed cynical and mocking, and over the four days of class, I began to wonder whether I belonged. I felt like a stranger in a strange land, as others seemed to question everything I placed my hope in. I don't know that I want to continue my studies at this seminary."

When I finished, the group, many of whom had walked with me from the beginning of the story of pursuing the degree, had questions and comments for me.

One woman reminded me that we tell our children that they won't always get along with a teacher. She asked me whether I really thought God wanted me to give up so quickly just because I'd had a negative experience with a professor.

Another woman observed, "It sounds like you did something you never would have done in the past. You voiced your beliefs. Even if you weren't heard by the professor or your classmates, you spoke up for what you believed, and that's very important."

The last to speak, a young woman relatively new to the group, gave me reason to continue in faith: "I haven't been in this group for very long, but since the beginning, the idea that God would call you to such a strange dream has encouraged me to consider that my calling, too, might be from God. Now I am seeing that moving into this mission may be fraught with trials, and that without a community that knows who God is and what he's done in my life, I'm sunk."

Touché. Our new friend summed up the whole purpose of story feasts—to help one another continue in faith by remembering the marvelous deeds that God has done and to encourage one another to wait in hope for God to do the impossible again. My friends called me to humble myself and to love God and others by living out his calling.

Everybody is a story. When I was a child, people sat around kitchen tables and told their stories. We don't do that so much anymore. Sitting around the table telling stories is not just a way of passing time. It is the way the wisdom gets passed along. The stuff that helps us to live a life worth remembering.

—Rachel Naomi Remen, *Kitchen-Table Wisdom*

STORY FEASTING

Sharing our stories is essential to growing in faith, hope, and love. As we hear the stories that others tell of how God has worked redemption in their lives, we often remember marvelous deeds that God has done in our own lives. In our telling stories of wrecked shalom, the Spirit often moves to grow our hope so that we can say, "This will make a really good story one day." Listening to others' stories draws us to know and love them in new ways. Sharing our own stories is a gift of love to other people.

"Okay," you may say, "I get why I need to share my story. But what's the deal with a feast?" The theme of feasting runs throughout God's story. God called his people to gather at appointed times to remember redemption and rescue in their lives. Everyone in the community participated in these feasts: the very young and the very old, the marginalized aliens and the community leaders. Traditional foods were an essential part of the feast; meat, bread, and wine were offered and enjoyed in thanksgiving to God.

In the Old Testament, the feast of Passover celebrated God's rescue of the Israelites from slavery in Egypt. In the New Testament, the Passover feast takes a strange turn when Christ says, "I tell you the truth, unless you eat the flesh of the Son of Man and drink his blood, you have no life in you. Whoever eats my flesh and drinks my blood has eternal life, and I will raise him up at the last day" (John 6:53-54). Now we remember the ultimate

[Paul] wants his story to result in deeper hope, strengthened faith, and renewed worship among them. . . . As people see God in Paul's story, they are given eyes to see God in their own, and they are comforted by this. . . . Our stories take God's truth to the struggles of life and present strong reasons not to give up.

—Paul David Tripp, *Instruments in the Redeemer's Hands*

rescue as we feast regularly on Christ's body and blood in the sacrament of Holy Communion.

As followers of Christ, we gather to offer our own stories to God and our community, naming both the tragedy and redemption of our narratives. Sharing our stories and hearing others' stories strengthens our faith, increases our hope, and compels us to move into a hurting world with love. Story feasting deepens the bonds of community and propels the mission of love that marks us as Christians.

You have a week to prepare for your story feast. Walk through the preparatory questions and get ready for the best feast you've ever experienced!

DAY 2

FOOD FOR THE FEAST

Feasts involve special foods. It may be a favorite treat you enjoy from the grocery store (double chocolate fudge chunk ice cream, anyone?), or it could be your dad's special barbecued rib recipe.

1. What "ritual food" will you share at the feast? What significance does it have for you?

Ground Rules

All feasts are governed by convention. Rules for story feasts help to ensure a safe and welcoming environment. The following five suggestions should help to build a foundation:

Tell your story purposefully. The main purpose of this story feast is to glorify God. Recognize that all sorts of stories glorify God in many different ways. This core purpose, however, does not mean that our stories have to be overly spiritual!

2. Think of a story that you like to tell. How might it draw others to see the beauty, majesty, humor, holiness, strength, kindness, or any other characteristic of God?

Tell your story honestly. Telling a story honestly means being willing to examine our own hearts. We have to open our hearts to hear what God and others have to say to us through the telling of the story. Ask the Holy Spirit to reveal more about who God is, who others are, or who you are in the telling of the story.

Tell your story honorably. Avoid the temptation toward gossip, slander, or vengeance in your stories. But don't avoid telling the truth or pretend that something cruel did not hurt you. Here is an example: I want to honor my parents always, but the reality is that their decision to divorce caused deep pain in my life. As long as I tell how I felt and don't stray to the topic of their mistakes or sinfulness, I am honoring my story and them. I may also tell a story publicly differently than I would tell it to my spouse, a trusted friend, or a counselor.

3. Think of a story of being harmed by someone. How could you tell that story honorably?

Listen to stories with integrity. We should seriously attend to others' stories. We should be willing to engage and always honor the privacy of the storyteller.

4. Have you experienced being listened to with integrity? What did the listener do to make you feel honored?

Take part. No one is required to tell a story (though it will be fairly dull if no one does). You are welcome to come and listen without the intent of sharing a story. But keep an open heart, because people often remember their own stories when they hear the stories of others.

DAY 3

Prepare the Story

Write the story.

1. Reread the story questions in the *Engaging Your Story* sections of the first two chapters.

2. Reread the stories you have written to respond to those questions. Choose one that you would like to work on some more and to share with the group.

3. Write it out if you haven't already.

DAY 4

Reflect on the Story

Consider any or all of the following questions:

1. What does this story reveal about you or others? What does it reflect about your style of relating to others?

2. What does this story show about who God is and what he has done?

3. Is there anything about the events of the story that makes you question the goodness of the heart of God? If so, take those questions to him in prayer. Review Psalm 77 for an excellent example of a psalmist crying out to God in confusion over the events of his life and the resultant reaffirmation of his faith.

4. What does the story reveal about sin, grace, or redemption?

5. Take your story to his story—the Word of God. Is there a story in the Bible that reminds you of yours? A character? A psalm?

DAY 5

Edit the Story

1. After reflecting on the questions above, rewrite where necessary.

   a. Take out details that aren't essential to the key point of the story.

   b. Add in details that would make the story clearer.

Share the Story

2. Each group member will be allotted about ten minutes for telling his or her story and hearing the thoughts of others. You can read a story that you have written, or you can tell the story from memory or by using an outline.

   a. Would you like to read or tell your story?

   b. If you are going to read the story, remember to engage your audience. Look at them and read it to them, expecting them to respond.

   c. If you are going to tell the story, make sure that you have the key points outlined. You've got only ten minutes, so it's important to focus on the essentials. Practice telling the story beforehand to see how long it takes.

Pull a thread in my story and feel the tremor half a world and two millennia away.

—Daniel Taylor, *Tell Me a Story: The Life-Shaping Power of Our Stories*

ℱINALLY, THE ℱEAST

Ideally, you should feast for about two and a half hours:

30 minutes: Feast and fellowship.

10 minutes: Leader introduces story theme and prays.

90 minutes (maximum): Story sharing. Ten minutes per person, so if your group is larger than nine people, divide into two smaller groups.

15 minutes: Close with a time of prayer for one another's stories.

DAY 6

Revisit the Story

Note: This is follow-up for after the feast. Think through it and jot some notes before the next meeting.

Revise the story. Consider the process of telling the story.

1. What kinds of responses did the group give you about your story?

2. How did you feel as you told your story?

3. Did you notice anything new about your story through the telling or through a group member's response?

4. Write down any specific prayers that you will pray for other group members based on the stories you heard.

Moving Forward

In the next chapter, we will focus more firmly on God as the conceiver and nurturer of hope as we consider the story of Sarah, a cynical woman who gives birth to laughter.

SARAH'S STORY

Struggling in Wait and Celebrating Surprise

KEY THEMES

- Like faith, hope is initiated by God and focuses on God's action. God is both the subject (initiator) and object (focus) of hope.

- Hope entails waiting, and the tension of waiting often causes us to struggle with God.

- Hope involves celebrating the hilarious surprise of God's scandalous grace.

DAY 1

Steve and Krista both heard it. On a sunny Sunday morning as a visiting pastor and his wife told about their church-planting journey, the young couple leaned forward in their seats, gripped by the story. That afternoon, Steve brought it up: "Krista, you know what that pastor said this morning?" Krista nodded. "Yeah,

I know. We need to go, don't we?" There was trepidation but no doubt. Together they heard God calling them to move into an uncertain future, promising them only that he would be with them along the way. And so began a long season of surrendering in trust and struggling in wait.

They both applied to seminary, he for pastoral training, she for counseling instruction. And they waited for acceptance.

Graduating from seminary, Steve and Krista attended church-planting assessment and were approved as a bright, hopeful couple ready to meet the rigors of ministry. And they waited for a call.

Six months later, the call came—to a church seven hundred miles away from their hometown. Their parents wondered whether it was a good idea to move so far away from their support system. And they waited for money to come to support their labor.

It took a year, but finally enough support had been raised for them to move and begin. They'd be eating a lot of ramen noodles, but they could go. They began meeting and planning with a core group of ten people who had expressed interest in being part of the team. And they waited for the site and time to hold their first service.

Three months after the core group began meeting, they had lost five of their members, three to a move and two to a divorce. They were discouraged and wondered whether they might have misheard God. And they waited. And they kept wondering.

In chapter 2, we learned that responding to God's call required Abraham to leave and let go of things that mattered deeply to him. Now we will look at his wife, Sarai/Sarah, the woman chosen to give birth to the promised son. A beautiful but barren "princess" whose story is weighty with suffering wait and surprising hope, Sarah will become the mother of multitudes.

Note: As we mentioned in chapter 2, Sarah's name, which means "princess," changes from *Sarai* to *Sarah* during the story. We will use *Sarah* throughout.

To wait on without surrendering the vision can be an exacting task.

—Derek Kidner, *Genesis*

ENGAGING SCRIPTURE: HEBREWS; GENESIS

For the background of Hebrews, please see the description in chapter 1. For the background of Genesis, please see the description in chapter 2.

As we trace the growth of Sarah's hope, we will look at three important chapters of her life:

- Chapter 1: Refusing to Wait
- Chapter 2: Laughing at Hope
- Chapter 3: Surprised by Hilarious Grace

Before we examine these, let's begin with an overview.

1. Read Hebrews 11:11, Genesis 11:29–31, and Genesis 12:1–11.

   a. What essential information do we learn about Sarah?

   b. What connection do you see between barrenness and hope?

   c. Read Genesis 12:1-5. What was Sarah's role in Abraham's initial call?

In chapter 2, we learned of Abraham's colossal failure of faith in two events when he passed Sarah off as his sister rather than his wife. In those stories, the narrator does not tell us what Sarah is thinking.

⚘ Choose a verse to memorize from any of the passages in this chapter. Write the verse here and tell why you chose it.

DAY 2

CHAPTER 1: REFUSING TO WAIT (GENESIS 16)

When shalom is broken and we are tired of waiting for God's promises to be fulfilled, we are often tempted to take control and create shalom on our own terms. In this catastrophic scene, we see Sarah and Abraham flee from faith and hope by foolishly devising their own plan to fulfill God's promise.

1. Read Genesis 16:1-3.

   a. What is wrong with the plan?

   b. How does it remind you of the breakdown of shalom (harmony and order) in Genesis 3?

2. Read Galatians 4:22-29.

   a. How does the apostle Paul use the Sarah-Hagar story to explain a crucial aspect of Christian faith?

Sarai-Sarah's first reported speech . . . is a complaint about childlessness. . . . Sarai's first two-sided dialogue with her husband (verses 5–6) vividly represents the first domestic squabble—her bitterness and resentment against the husband who, after all, has only complied with her request; his willingness to buy conjugal peace at almost any price.

—Robert Alter, *Genesis*

b. How are we as Christians similar to Abraham and Sarah? (On whom is our salvation dependent?)

3. Read Genesis 16:7-15. What hope do you see in the story of God's coming to Hagar?

74

In Genesis 16, we see Sarah, heroine of hope, scheming to bring God's promise in her way in her time, and Abraham, hero of faith, complying. The good news of God's story of grace is that he does not allow us to remain long in our narrow narratives.

As we learned in chapter 2, God reestablishes the covenant in Genesis 17, changing the names of Abraham and Sarah. Sarah's new name is an expansion of the first; in the same way, her role is expanded to include being the mother of multitudes.

Now we move to Genesis 18, where we observe an intimate, humorous, and compassionate encounter between the Lord and a somewhat cynical Sarah.

CHAPTER 2: LAUGHING AT HOPE (GENESIS 18)

1. Read Genesis 18:9-11.

   a. Why do you suppose the Lord speaks through Abraham to Sarah?

   b. In what new way is God's promise stated? How does this approach reveal God's kindness toward Sarah?

2. Read Genesis 18:12–14.

    a. What is Sarah's response? What are her reasons for disbelieving God's promise?

    b. Sarah has succumbed to cynicism. How does the Lord respond to her hopelessness?

3. Read Genesis 18:15.

    a. Sarah lies to God. How does God respond to her?

b. What does the Lord's response show about his love for us as sinners?

c. The story ends here. In what way is this ending somewhat surprising? In what way is it very true to how real life happens?

Sarah's story shows us that the laughter of faith is the laughter of incongruity. But ultimately, like Sarah and Abraham, real faith casts us wholeheartedly upon the God who is free to act and to do as God wants, in God's time, and in God's way. Faith is the ability to answer "yes" to the God for whom nothing is impossible, even when our lives tell us the answer is "no."

—Margaret Manning, "The Incongruity Theory of Faith"

They called him laughter
For he came after
The father had made an impossible promise come true
The birth of a baby to a hopeless old lady
So they called him laughter
Cause no other name would do.

—Michael Card, "They Called Him Laughter"

Sarah has settled into the safe, familiar wasteland of despair. Certain that she will never conceive a child, she finds the prospect of arousing hope dangerous and terrifying. God approaches her gently and intimately, seeing into her heart and inviting her to laugh with astonishment at the story of grace that he is writing. Again, the Bible emphasizes that the sustainer of our hope is God.

⚙ Practice your memory verse by writing it on social media or in a note or e-mail.

DAY 3

SURPRISED BY HILARIOUS GRACE

And they lived happily ever after. Or not. The promised "ending" to the story arrives with the baby Isaac, whose name means "laughter." In this chapter, we see Sarah laughing at the hilarity of God's ways.

1. Read Genesis 21:1–3.

   a. What do these verses show us about the nature of hope?

b. Why did Abraham name Isaac as he did (Gen. 17:19)?

Theological Theme: Eschatology

My hope is built on nothing less than Jesus' blood and righteousness.
>   —Edward Mote, "My Hope Is Built on Nothing Less"

Eschatology is a big word that means the "study of last things"; in Christianity, it specifically refers to the "divinely ordained climax of the end of history."* For the Christian, hope is based on the fulfilled promises of God in Christ's resurrection (1 Cor. 15:12–19) and ultimately on Christ's return to restore all things fully (1 Peter 1:13).

Throughout the Bible, we are called to hope because of what God will do in the final chapter (Rom. 8:25; 2 Cor. 5:17). In addition, as followers of Christ, we cannot escape hope. God pursued Sarah in her cynicism and hopelessness; the Holy Spirit lives in our hearts, pumping hope through our lifeblood, even when we do not feel it: those who hope for the messianic age are "prisoners of hope" (Zech. 9:12).

As Christians, we are pilgrims of hope, fixing our eyes on a day when we live in full glory with Christ our Savior (Heb. 11:13). When we fix our eyes on end times (the eschaton), we more easily recognize our tendency to focus our hope on idols that bring only temporary shalom: a strong economy, a date every night, or an A on the biology exam. The great hope of our future is that we will be renewed fully to live giving glory to God: "We shall be like him, for we shall see him as he is" (1 John 3:2).

* Douglas Harper, "eschaton. Dictionary.com. Online Etymology Dictionary," *Dictionary.com*, 1935, http://dictionary.reference.com/browse/eschaton.

Epilogue (Genesis 21:8–21)

The Bible rarely leaves us with fairy-tale endings, and within a few years, Sarah's laughter changes to anger when she hears Ishmael mocking her son, Isaac. In this strange vignette, God tells Abraham to do what Sarah says (a strong departure from Genesis 16). God treasures Ishmael, but Isaac is God's chosen son, and Ishmael refuses to bow down before him. In Galatians 4, we are reminded that the only hope for salvation is bowing before another promised Son, the Messiah.

⚙ Review your memory verse by posting it on social media or writing it in a note or an e-mail.

DAY 4

ENTERING YOUR STORY

As Christians, we are waiting for delivery—the day when all things will be made new as they were meant to be. Meanwhile, we struggle with glory and grace. At times, we, like Sarah and Abraham, try to make life work on our own terms; other times, we wait patiently, believing God against all signs of earthly impossibility. Read this story written by my lovely friend so aptly named Hope, and think about how hope operates in your life.

Hope's long season of loss began with the death of the "darling" of the high school in a tragic car accident. She writes of "the day the music died":

At my first experience of deep sorrow and loss, I questioned God: Why had he allowed this to happen, and why to her? Couldn't it have been someone who wasn't so influential in my life? God's hope only arrived in more suffering. The fabric of my security, already frayed by Liz's death, was soon ripped to shreds.

I am a preacher's daughter. Our family had arrived only three years before as my father accepted the pastorate of the biggest church in this small town. Most of the congregation were life-long members, and had been shepherded for twenty-eight years by a dear man who finally resigned because of failing health. Soon after we arrived, he passed away, but his family remained, committed to controlling the church.

An excited, eager pastor, ready to breathe new life into a spiritually dying church, came to a people who were comfortable in their tradition and resistant to a change in leadership. Can you see the disaster cocktail brewing? People took sides. They wanted Dad gone, and to get him out they exchanged the truth for lies. Sunday school teachers who had shared God's Word with me, who had loved me, and whom I had trusted became the betrayers hurling accusations at my father. This sour potion of religion left a horrible aftertaste of church lingering long.

It became clear that we couldn't stay, so at the Sunday evening business meeting when his resignation was called for, my father gave it. It was a brutal night. I remember the sick feeling—the mental anguish of hypocrisy before me, the knot in my stomach as my world was ripped in two. The following day at school as I told Lisa the news, I felt numb. And so as she cried for me, I could not. The music of my life was muffled by the pain of tragedy. I no longer cared to sing in the halls. My soul could not smile.

We survived the spring, staying long enough to complete the school year, and for Dad to find someplace for us to go. I would frequently see our betrayers around town, and each time, my heart would harden a little more. *They* were to blame for this awful mess we were in.

In that story, I struggled to hope. But God had a new song awaiting us in San Antonio, Texas. My father took a call as an army chaplain, and we entered a big world (we were in Texas, after all), complete with a *big* church and a *big* high school where we were able to be embraced for ourselves and find healing.

Music, a lifelong passion, took on a new dimension for me. It became the outlet for my heartache, as I poured myself with renewed fervor into my piano and vocal training. A first-class high school choir brought new bonds of community and friendship. As God used these instruments to heal my broken heart, I was able to let go of the bitterness and resentment and find forgiveness for those who had caused us such pain. As I healed, God resurrected the song of my heart: "He put a new song in my mouth, a hymn of praise to our God" (Ps. 40:3a).

1. Tell a story about a time when you were "surprised by hope" after a long wait.

    a. What struggles with believing the impossible did you experience as you waited? Did you ever look to idols to create a sense of shalom?

    b. How did the waiting affect your relationship with God?

2. Psalm 88 is a powerful psalm, seemingly devoid of hope. And yet hope is found in the fact that the psalmist is still crying out to God in his despair. Read this beautiful psalm of lament and write a psalm, prayer, poem, or song or create a visual image of a story of doubt, confusion, or despair in your life.

⚘ Review your memory verse. Say it aloud two times.

Hope cannot be separated from its gut realities. We think of hope as something "out there" that we either find or lose. The reality is, hope is something that rises up inside of us with a gentle strength that requires a response. We either respond to it with our hearts or we try to push it down. Responding to it brings a deepened sense of thirst, a deepened ache.

—Jan Meyers, *The Allure of Hope*

DAY 5

LIVING STORY

As we await the *eschaton* (the end of this world), we encounter many evidences of the fall. Look at the list below and check the broken "stories" that interest you. Dan Allender describes hope as a "vision of redemption in the midst of decay."[1] Write one sentence that expresses such a hope for you. Put a star by any in which you are or would like to be involved.

☐ Orphans
  Example: I desire that all children would know the care of a parent.
  I went on a mission trip to an orphanage and will do it again.
☐ Global economy
☐ Sustainability (agriculture, farming)
☐ Marriage
☐ Poverty
☐ Sex trafficking of women and children
☐ Church

PRAYING STORY

Choose any story from the *Entering Your Story* or *Living Story* section of this chapter and write a prayer surrendering any fear or doubt to God and asking him to reveal his hilarious hope in one of these areas.

Alternatively, write a prayer of praise and thanksgiving for how God has moved with scandalous grace in one of the difficult stories of your life.

1. Dan Allender and Tremper Longman III, *Cry of the Soul* (Colorado Springs: Navpress, 1995), 155.

Moving Forward

What a story! Sarah, weary of waiting for God to fulfill the promise, tries to build shalom on her own terms. God graciously allows her to fail. Later, when her shriveled body gives her no reason to believe that her barren womb will ever fill, Sarah attempts to give up hoping. Through it all, God makes his point clear: he is a God who fulfills promises. He will do far more than we ever ask or imagine, though often we must wait to see what that looks like. Let's turn to God's birthing of even more surprising promised sons in the New Testament to learn more about living in faith and hope.

5

MARY'S STORY

Resting in Trust and Wrestling with Redemption

KEY THEMES

- Faith is strengthened by the remembrance of redemption.
- Surrendering in trust brings rest.
- Restlessness results when we try to fit redemption into our own categories.

DAY 1

Here we return to the story told in chapter 1 by Heather:

A year after Knox died, my husband and I were preparing for a much-needed getaway to Santiago, Chile. Then we received the shocking news that my older brother, my only sibling, had died in his sleep at the age of forty-three. We changed our flight plans and flew to Houston instead of Santiago.

As I struggled to process the news, the grief spilled into my soul. I thought, "You can do this. You can walk this path because you have seen Jon and Rachel walk their path, and others as well. It is a hard path, but not impossible because the Lord will take you. He has promised to walk with you."

On the day of my brother's service, several of our church friends made the hour drive to come alongside me in my family's grief. The last time I had seen them was the year before as we grieved for Knox. Even Knox's dad came—I couldn't imagine how difficult it would be for him to attend a funeral just a year after his son's. My heart swelled with gratitude.

Afterward, back at my mother's house, my mom asked quietly, "Was Knox's dad there?"

"Yes," I said. She nodded her head gently and turned away as tears filled our eyes.

"Yes," I thought, "he was there as a witness to the Lord who promises to never leave or forsake us, who promises to walk with us through our suffering and grief. We are not alone in this, and we never will be—in this and in the things to come."

My friend Heather's story shows how faith empowers us to step with hope into the uncertain and seemingly impossible call of God. In this chapter, we explore yet another story of God's hilarious grace: the birth of *the* promised Son through a virgin. Mary, the mother of Jesus, is offered one simple yet profound sentence on which to hang her hope: "Nothing is impossible with God" (Luke 1:37). In the early chapters of Mary's story, her submission to God's call shows how the surrender of trust results in rest. Later, however, she displays the restlessness that results when we confine redemption to our cramped categories.

God, you have made us for yourself, and our hearts are restless until they find their rest in thee.

—Augustine of Hippo, *Confessions*

ENGAGING SCRIPTURE: LUKE 1; LUKE 2:41-52

Background

Genre. Gospel. The *gospel*, from the Greek word *euangelion*, meaning "good news," specifically refers to the story of salvation in Jesus Christ. Though each of the four Gospels (Matthew, Mark, Luke, and John) is tailored to a different audience, they all record Jesus' life and his spoken words.

Context. Luke, the author, experienced marginalization as a Gentile in a largely Jewish culture. Because his Gospel offers a unique perspective on Jesus as the Lord of the disenfranchised, it features stories of women, common laborers, Samaritans, and the poor. Luke provides an inside look at the struggle of faith and hope endured by Mary, the mother of the Savior.

Before we launch into Mary's story, let's consider the pre-amble—the story of Zechariah. In Luke 1:5-25, a priest named Zechariah has his once-in-a-lifetime opportunity to make the offering inside the temple. Something astonishing and yet really not surprising at all happens when he enters—an angel shows up. Zechariah is terrified; he had not been expecting to meet a messenger of God.

The angel's words unnerve him even more: "Do not be afraid, Zechariah; your prayer has been heard. Your wife Elizabeth will bear you a son" (Luke 1:13). Zechariah's wife, Elizabeth, is barren, and they have been praying for a baby for years. The angel goes on to name the child (John) and describe him in vast detail, describing his lifestyle (drinking no wine or beer), his heart (filled with the Holy Spirit), and his mission (calling the Israelites to turn back to God).

Zechariah's response? He asks, in utter disbelief, "How can I be sure of this? I am an old man and my wife is well along in years" (Luke 1:18). Zechariah's faith fails him, and his hope goes missing. He seems to forget the redemption story that he has told and lived as an Israelite priest.

When presented with the call to faith, the offer of hope, Sarah laughs and Zechariah questions. To Sarah, God answers with gentle invitation; to Zechariah, God provides silence. Both are gracious responses that foster confidence in God's promises. Now we turn to Mary's story to see how remembering redemption in community nurtures the calm assurance of faith and hope.

 ❋ Choose a memory verse from the Scripture in this chapter. Write it here and tell why you chose it.

DAY 2

We will look at three chapters in Mary's story to see how Mary rests in God and wrestles with redemption.

 ❋ Chapter 1: Resting in Trust
 ❋ Chapter 2: Wrestling with Redemption
 ❋ Chapter 3: Resting in Redemption

CHAPTER 1: RESTING IN TRUST

1. Read Luke 1:26–33. Pretend that you are a news reporter describing the scene of the angel Gabriel's visit to Mary.

   a. Write a paragraph summarizing the events of verses 26–33.

   b. What does this interaction reveal about the relationship between grace and faith?

   c. In what ways does the angel's announcement wreck Mary's current shalom?

2. Read Luke 1:34–38.

    a. How is Mary's question like and unlike Zechariah's (Luke 1:18, 34)?

    b. Gabriel offers three different responses to Mary's question (vv. 35, 36, and 37). What are they, and which would you find most helpful?

c. Read verses 37–38 aloud. Review Hebrews 11:1. What does this interaction reveal about the call and response of faith and hope? What do you learn about the rest that comes from surrendering in trust?

3. Read Luke 1:39–45. What does Mary's visit with Elizabeth reveal about the importance of community in sustaining faith and hope?

4. Read Luke 1:46–56. In this redemption song, Mary remembers God's story of grace. Let's look at three particular themes she sings.

a. What does Mary recognize about her personal story (vv. 46–49)?

Mary's prayer takes us into an expansive world of God's promises that are in the process of being fulfilled. Prayer enlarges our imagination and makes us grateful, joyful participants in what has been and what is yet to come.

—Eugene Peterson, *Conversations: The Message with Its Translator*

b. What does the song say about the surprising nature of grace (vv. 51–55)?

c. What specific story does Mary mention that might sustain her faith and hope in her current circumstances (vv. 54–55)?

❋ Review your memory verse by sharing it on social media or sending it in a letter to a friend.

DAY 3

CHAPTER 2: WRESTLING WITH REDEMPTION

Read Luke 2:41-52. In this story, we see Mary struggling to live in faith and hope as her Son refuses to limit himself to her categories of redemption. Here, worry and disbelief unsettle the rest of shalom.

1. During the annual pilgrimage to Jerusalem for the Passover Feast, Jesus exercises his authority as God the Son and stays behind to teach in the temple.

    a. How does community and communication break down in the beginning of this story (vv. 41–44)?

    b. Imagine being Mary or Joseph during the three days in which they do not know the whereabouts of their Son. What happens to you when you are required to wait on something very important to you?

2. The Greek word in verse 48 is *odynomenoi*, meaning "deep anguish and distress."

   a. What causes Mary's deep anguish and distress (v. 48)?

   b. How does Jesus answer her? In what way do you see an invitation to repentance in Jesus' response (v. 49)?

   c. Why do you think Mary and Joseph do not understand what Jesus is saying to them (v. 50)?

3. Read Luke 2:51–52.

   a. How does this story reveal Jesus' nature as fully human and fully God (v. 51)?

b. How does Mary's heart change from the beginning of the story to the end?

CHAPTER 3: RESTING IN REDEMPTION

In one of the most painful scenes of Mary's life, she stands with others beholding her Son, the Messiah, naked, beaten, bloodied, and hanged on a cross for the entire world to mock. This moment appears to be the culmination of Simeon's foretelling: "a sword will pierce your own soul" (Luke 2:35). Let's look at these final moments to see how Jesus brings rest to his mother's heart.

1. Read John 19:25–27. How would entrusting John to Mary and Mary to John provide hope for both of them in the coming days?

We are not told that she said anything as she stood at the foot of the cross. Jesus, we are told, gives her the beloved disciple to care for her in his place. She is about to have another three days of agony, mourning the loss of Israel's hope and consolation, another three days before love's bright pain will fill her life, as once before it filled her body, not of the will of man, but of God.

—N. T. Wright, *The Crown and the Fire*

2. What do we learn in Acts 1:14 about Mary's faith and hope?

Theological Theme: Rest

We have seen Mary rest when she surrenders control of her life to God; we have seen her wrestle when she tries to force redemption to fit her narrow framework. Rest is the outcome of faith and hope in Jesus Christ.

Mary's words, "I am the Lord's servant. . . . May it be to me as you have said" (Luke 1:38), reveal the quiet strength described in Isaiah 30:15. Her worry and distress over Jesus' disappearance demonstrate the frenzied anxiety and restlessness that result from a lack of trust and an unwillingness to wait. As Jesus invites her to repent and she "treasure[s] . . . these things in her heart" (Luke 2:51), Mary returns to a state of rest.

In our overworked Western world, where manic schedules seem to signify higher status, we often ignore or disdain rest. Scripture makes it clear that rest is not a luxury—it is a calling. God created it (Gen. 2:2–3), and he commands it (Ex. 20:8–11). In turning back to God as the only source of salvation, we receive rest (Isa. 30:15). Rest is the promised state of those who say no to self-salvation (Heb. 4). It is our way of life as well as our end of life. When Christ returns, shalom will be completely restored, and all who trust in him will finally and fully rest.

Believers experience rest in the gospel, acknowledging that Christ's work alone is sufficient to atone for our sins. When we cease striving from our efforts to save ourselves by legalism or human merit, we rest in the knowledge that God is God and we are not.

DAY 4

ᴇNTERING ᴏYOUR STORY

Mary's story begins and ends in submission to God's will, but she wavers between full surrender and restless struggle. Like Mary, we all have times when surrendering to God and embracing his rest come only through hard wrangling. One of my "wrangling stories" is about the long, arduous recovery from shoulder surgery. Journal excerpts reveal the restlessness of my soul:

February 2011
Again this past week, my heart has been turbulent, like the weaned child throwing a temper tantrum in the grocery store aisle because my mama won't buy me a supersize bag of animal crackers. Or maybe a family-size bag of snack carrots, because, after all, what I'm longing for isn't bad for me. All I want is for my shoulder to heal fully, to be pain-free with normal use. All I want is not to require another surgery.

The tantrum usually goes something like this: "I'm getting better, but there's something wrong. I feel it. WHAT'S THE POINT?! Why am I still in PT? Why is that frail elderly lady next to me doing so much better when she's only three months out, and I'm almost seven months out? I'm going to do all this and then just have to have the procedure that they should have done in the first place."

This raging is clearly the opposite of the "my heart is not too haughty nor too lofty" idea in Psalm 131 and exposes my sense of entitlement.

A great benefit of Sabbath keeping is that we learn to let God take care of us—not by becoming passive and lazy, but in the freedom of giving up our feeble attempts to be God in our own lives.

—Marva Dawn, *Keeping the Sabbath Wholly*

March 2011

(On this morning, I spied condensation in the window where I kneel to pray—no big deal, except that it was heart-shaped!)

"As for you, God, your way is perfect, your Word is proven. You are a shield to all who take refuge in You.... Who is our Rock besides You, O God?" (Ps. 18:30–31).

A condensation heart. A condensed heart. Right there before my very face, making the heart of God "my-size"—large enough not to be ignored, small enough that it fits in two windowpanes, misshapen enough that it seems just right for me, inexplicably there—condensation, sure—in a heart-shape on the window where I go to pray—huh??? There is no other condensation on that window. And as of this writing, fifteen minutes after I first saw it, it is still there.

God there, in my window, telling me that he loves me.

Opening my daily prayer book to find love sprinkled liberally through all the passages.

I love you, my daughter: "Daughter, your faith has healed you; now go in peace."

Calling me to affirm this word from Scripture: "As for you, God, your way is perfect, your Word is proven" (Ps. 18:30).

Bringing me to voice these words: "Lord, I surrender this shoulder to you. I surrender healing or not-healing. It is yours to do with as you will. I surrender my capacity to understand why. I surrender the desire to blame—it is not my fault that it's not better yet. It is not because the doctor or physical therapist is doing something wrong."

Your way is perfect, and your love is perfect.

September 2011

It is easier to write about now. I have had that second surgery, and in the last month, motion has returned swiftly, and pain has decreased gradually. Hope is surging. And yet I am hopeful for more than my shoulder. I am seeing the strength of God's pursuit of my heart, how he wants my heart to be surrendered to him, to trust him that he is good, in healing and not-healing. God has favored me in this story all along, though I am just now beginning to believe it.

1. Tell of a time when you struggled to understand God's ways and timing in redemption.

   a. What "signs of grace," if any, did you see?

   b. What previous stories of redemption, if any, did you remember, or were you reminded of?

2. Tell a "story of rest," a season (or a moment) of shalom when your heart was at rest with God, a time when you

enjoyed God and others deeply, when you knew God's delight in you and rejoiced in it.

a. How did rest come? (Did it follow a hard season, or was it a planned celebration, or something else?)

b. What did you understand about the heart of God? How did you celebrate or share the shalom with others?

⬤ Review your memory verse.

DAY 5

LIVING STORY

1. Read Revelation 21 and 22. Plan a day of joy and rest.

   a. What elements will it include? (Consider setting, people, food, and any other necessary elements.)

   b. How will this "sabbath" be a foretaste of the complete joy found in Revelation 21 and 22?

   c. Choose a day to enact this rest and do it. Later, write about how it went.

Sabbath is our re-creating the garden and recreating in the new heavens and earth.

—Dan Allender, *Sabbath*

PRAYING STORY

2. Read Mary's redemption song, Luke 1:46-55, aloud. If you'd like, write your own prayer based on this song.

Moving Forward

We have learned much so far on our journey of faith and hope. Faith derives from the gracious favor of God; it does not depend on our works. Hope focuses on the promise of rest to be consummated at the end of God's story. Now we will look at the "end of the story," the hope of the full inheritance that is ours in Christ Jesus.

6

THE HERO'S STORY

Seeing the Unseen: Faith and Hope Fulfilled

KEY THEMES

- Faith and hope rest ultimately on the as-yet-unseen reality of the new heavens and the new earth.

- Worship, our supreme calling, is the sum of a life of faith, hope, and love.

DAY 1

My friend Stephanie worked with a small group of men and women to write a vision plan for their church. The vision described a church centered in gospel growth, empowered by the Holy Spirit, and marked by relationships revealing the reconciling heart of God. It called their church to move out in kingdom mission to invite others to know the hope of Jesus Christ.

"It was a lovely plan, described in details that could be lived out. We believed God would make it happen," she said.

If we have faith in God's willingness to act on our behalf, it's possible to wait for him to act. And the waiting isn't a waiting of anxiety but a waiting of anticipation. It's based on the certainty that God is coming.

—Eugene Peterson, *Conversations: The Message with Its Translator*

The church gathered around the vision plan and began implementing it with excitement and anticipation. Within the first year, everyone could see the vision becoming reality. But then a strange thing happened. The governing board made an inexplicable decision that halted movement and, in fact, took the church in an entirely different direction from the stated vision. Arguments began, bitter words flew, and fractures spread. Six months later, after laboring to stay united with the church they loved, Stephanie, along with several other leaders of the vision committee, left, without seeing their hopes, which they believed to be God's plan, fulfilled.

Our study of the stories of Abraham, Sarah, and Mary has revealed the struggle of faith and hope. As Christians, we live in the era of the already/not-yet, anticipating the day that Christ will come again to rule and reign forever on this renewed earth. We've heard tales of the story's ending (Isa. 11; 60; 65; 2 Peter 3; Rev. 21–22), and we know they're true. Like the heroes of faith, we can see full restoration from afar, drawing us toward a life beyond this fallen and partially redeemed earth. The final wait of faith and hope is for an eternal life of worship that our hearts were designed for.

ENGAGING SCRIPTURE: HEBREWS 11:13–40; ISAIAH 65:17–25

Background

Genre. (For Hebrews, see chapter 1.) Prophecy. Most biblical prophecy emphasizes "declaring the word" of God and calling people to return to their Creator. Isaiah contains these elements as well as prophecy predicting the future. Isaiah is a beautifully written, highly literary masterpiece, composed of many genres, such as poetry, history, biography, and apocalyptic literature.

Context. Isaiah focuses on the God who has saved in the past and will definitively do so in the future. With a strong emphasis on God's holiness, and a foretelling of Jesus as Messiah, Servant, and King, it calls the people of Israel to repent and worship God. The final section of Isaiah focuses on the reason for hope, a final day when restoration will be complete.

Faith and Hope: Seeing the Far-Off Country

Read Hebrews 11:13–16 and 11:32–40.

1. As we learned in our first study, many of the heroes of faith named in Hebrews 11 experienced, "by faith," God's promised redemption. They also endured suffering as they waited. Read Hebrews 11:32–40.

   a. What are some of the promises fulfilled in the heroes' stories (vv. 32–35)?

b. What suffering did they endure (vv. 35–38)?

2. Read Hebrews 11:13–16 and 39–40.

a.   What promises have the heroes of faith not yet received?

b. How does verse 14 describe the nature of faith and hope (review Hebrews 11:1)?

3. Read Hebrews 11:8-16. The Greek word used for *foreigner* is *xenoi*, a derogatory term meaning "alien" or "outsider." The Greek word for *stranger* is *parapedemoi*, meaning "sojourner," one who lives temporarily in a place.

   a. What is the life of a foreigner and stranger on earth, according to verses 8-16?

   b. In what ways do you feel like a foreigner or a stranger in this world? In what ways do you think you might be too comfortable?

4. Read Hebrews 12:1-3.

   a. Who makes up the "great cloud of witnesses"?

The existential power of faith made the distant hope a reality, and these believers of the ancient world "saw" and "greeted" the promised consummation, even . . . in the hour of death, as though face to face with it.

—Philip Edgcumbe Hughes, *A Commentary on the Epistle to the Hebrews*

---

b. What verbs describe what we must do to live a life of faith and hope?

c. What does it mean that Jesus is the "author and perfecter of our faith"?

❂ Choose a memory verse and tell why you chose it.

DAY 2

THE PROMISE FULFILLED

In part 1 of the Living Story series, we studied the consummation of the kingdom described in Revelation 21 and 22. With the heroes of faith, we must keep the vision of that as-yet-unseen city before us in order to live a life of faith and hope. Let's look at another description of the certain shalomed life we await in Isaiah 65:17–25.

Read Isaiah 65:17–25.

1. Verse 18 begins with a command to the audience, which now includes us, to be glad and rejoice.

   a. What reasons for rejoicing does the rest of the passage describe (vv. 18–19)?

   b. The answer to question 1 of the Westminster Shorter Catechism states: "Man's chief end is to glorify God, and to enjoy Him for ever." What do you think it means to "enjoy" God?

2. Promises fulfilled:

    a. In what ways are the particular struggles of Abraham, Sarah, and Mary addressed in the New Jerusalem (vv. 20-24)?

    b. In what way is the new creation the perfect fulfillment of the promises that the other heroes of faith saw from afar?

3. Shalom restored:

    a. How are the effects of the fall reversed in the new heavens? How is shalom fully restored?

We live in a fallen world, where things and people fall apart. That's reality—and reality is often painful, when those who suffer and die are our loved ones. But the Christian recognizes a reality beyond this reality, a world beyond this world, a story beyond history. He or she knows by faith that the painful reality that we see all around us will one day pass away. It will be replaced by a world in which God will dwell with his people, in which he will wipe away every tear from their eyes, and where there will be no more death or mourning or crying or pain (Rev. 21:3–4).

—Iain Duguid, *Living in the Gap between Promise and Reality*

---

b. Which of the images of perfected shalom is particularly appealing to you in this season of your life?

❀ Review your memory verse by posting it on social media or sending it in a note to a friend.

DAY 3

Theological Theme: Worship

Life in the holy city, the New Jerusalem, will be characterized by perfect worship, all of creation bowing down before the Creator. Worship, says John Piper, is not "a mythical interlude in a week of reality."* Rather, it is a daily choosing to fix our hope on Jesus as the author and perfecter of our salvation, to surrender in trust to a holy and sovereign God, telling and living his good-news story in the world.

The words for worship in both Hebrew and Greek mean "to prostrate oneself, to bow down." Picture a servant approaching a king, kneeling and then planting his forehead on the ground. To worship is to assume a humble position. We all make choices moment by moment about whom or what we will serve. Adam and Eve served their own desires, dismissing God's, when they disobeyed by eating the fruit. Abraham worshiped God by offering his most precious possession, believing by faith that God would provide a rescue.

The Westminster Shorter Catechism describes the chief purpose of humankind: "to glorify God and to enjoy Him for ever." Scotty Smith explains that we were designed to live life to the glory of God, for and in the pleasure of God. Dan Allender says that worship is a cycle of enjoyment based on our understanding that we do not deserve to dance with God, and yet, by his grace, we do. God takes delight in us, and we take delight in him (Zeph. 3:14–17). Isaiah 65:18 emphasizes the delight of praising God, telling us to "be glad and rejoice forever in what [God] will create."

One day, God will dwell with us (Rev. 21) and worship will be characterized by the harmony and flourishing of perfected relationships. We live as worshipers now in anticipation of the day when we will delight ourselves fully in the glory of God.

* John Piper, lecture (Pensacola Theological Institute, August 1995).

Let us worship as a Bride whose "citizenship is in heaven," one who "eagerly await[s] a Savior from there, the Lord Jesus Christ" (Phil. 3:20). Let us love as a people who are looking forward to the Day of international knee bending and cosmic transformation—when every tongue will humbly confess and everything in God's new creation will loudly sing that Jesus Christ is Lord, to the glory of God the Father. Amen!

—Scotty Smith, *The Reign of Grace*

ENTERING YOUR STORY

"Monday," a short story by Mark Helprin, describes a man who experiences worship of the Creator anew as he partakes in a spectacular renovation. In the story, a contractor accepts the job of restoring an old New York City apartment for the widow of a man killed in the South Tower on September 11, 2001. Without her knowledge, the contractor decides to do the work for free, and a remarkable work of art is created as his laborers join with him in this self-sacrificial gift. Helprin describes the restoration project:

The work itself became the object and never in their lives had they done better. Never had the walls been straighter or smoother, never had the plaster been whiter, never had the wood been closer joined, never had the joints been tighter, the colors more intense, the proportions more artful. . . . When they fitted it all in . . . the men kept on saying, "Look at that! Look at that!" because nowhere in New York or perhaps anywhere was there a better job. . . . This was repeated in the rosewood paneling, in limestone baseboards, in nickel, marble, granite, and unobtrusive plaster molding that physics said could not be whiter, purer, or more like snow in bright sun. It was apparent in the ironwork, brasswork, and glazing. The solid walnut doors were two and a half inches thick, with the same brass hardware and hinges as in the White House, and they closed more smoothly and quietly than the doors of a Rolls-Royce.[1]

The contractor, as he watches this marvelous transformation, understands worship as never before, when he attended Mass:

> The mass existed, in his perhaps heretical view, to keep, encourage, and sustain a sense of holiness, and to hold open the channels to grace that, with age and discouragement, tend to close. Witness to those who had little sacrificing what they had, to their children contributing to the work in their way, and to the fathers' pride in this, Fitch felt the divine presence as he had not since the height of his youth.[2]

As we anticipate the day when we will see God's restoration project completed, we worship by playing a part in his redemption plan. Consider the following questions to contemplate your stories of worship and re-creation:

1. Tell a story of seeing God's grace in creation (a sunset, a shark, a work of art, music, sports—consider all possibilities). What aspects of God did you see anew? How did this glimpse of glory draw you to worship?

1. Mark Helprin, "Monday," in *The Pacific and Other Stories* (New York: Penguin, 2004), 68.
2. Ibid., 67.

2. Review Isaiah 65:17–25. Think of a hard story in your life that connects to one of the images of perfected shalom in the holy city. (For example: a woman struggling with infertility might be intrigued by the idea of no more barrenness; some might be encouraged by the idea that their labor will not be in vain.)

   a. What transformation did you see? What beauty was created?

b. How did you see God use you as a redeemed redeemer?

c. In what ways did you experience the chief end of humankind: glorifying God and enjoying him forever?

d. Write an imagined ending of what that broken place will look like when it is fully redeemed.

DAY 4

LIVING STORY

1. The passage in Isaiah also tells us that prejudice and racism, poverty, injustice, and oppression will be gone in the new heavens and the new earth.

   a. What are some particular concerns of your community that you would like to see eradicated (environment, racism, sexism, orphans, abuse, domestic violence, education, corruption, etc.)?

   b. Write a description of the transformation you'd like to see. How can you be an agent of hope in this story?

c. Write down two actions you can take and the date by which you will have taken them.

⚙ Review your memory verse by reading or saying it aloud several times.

DAY 5

ᎧPRAYING STORY

Dear God, Fulfiller of Faith, Restorer of Hope,

We come to you humbly, confessing that we so often want your promises to be fulfilled in our time and in our way. We thank you that you are God and we are not, that you refuse to bow to our demands, but that you instead draw us to kneel at your majesty, to declare your wonder, to marvel at your beauty. Help us to walk as the heroes of faith, fixing our eyes on your heavenly city from afar, remembering your "already" redemption, and knowing with deep assurance that you are redeeming and transforming now. You will never stop until the day Christ returns to fulfill your greatest promise. In hope assured by you and faith founded in you, we pray. Amen.

Moving Forward

What a wondrous journey it's been. Through floundering faith and struggling hope we have come to see that Jesus, the perfecter of our faith, gives us eyes to see our future hope and hearts to stay in the battle now. Before we conclude, we must share our stories in a feast proclaiming the glorious grace of God.

7

A WORSHIP FESTIVAL

KEY THEMES

- ✦ Living a story of faith and hope culminates in loving, serving, and worshiping God.

- ✦ When Christ returns, we will see him as he really and truly is (1 John 3:2), and our assurance of God's grace will never waver. Until that day, we tell our stories to remember God's rescue and dream of the day when we will join with all creation in worshiping perfectly.

DAY 1

Now faith is the assurance of things hoped for, the conviction of things not seen. (Heb. 11:1 ESV)

They died without receiving the promises. (Heb 11:13, paraphrased)

They saw the city from afar. (Heb. 11:13, paraphrased)

At this point, I pray, our understanding of faith and hope has deepened and widened to encompass the unseen realities and riches that we inherit, both now and later, in Christ Jesus. Let's briefly review what we've learned. Faith, the gift of God, comes with a call, and responding to that call requires letting go of things that give us a fleeting sense of relief. Hope in God sustains faith, leading us to persevere through suffering and uncertainty, even or especially when God's redemption plan doesn't seem to fit our categories. Laughter at the surprise of God's hilarious grace and celebration of his kindness are natural responses for the faithful and hopeful. Surrendering in trust and waiting in hope lead to the ultimate callings of a Christian's life: rest and worship. Most importantly, faith and hope were designed to be lived in community, not alone.

As we have seen in this series, God has written his love in Scripture, and he has also etched his grace uniquely into each of our individual stories. These are the stories we celebrate. As we await the final feast in the new heavens and the new earth, we gather to remember our stories now. Remembering both tragedy and redemption sustains faith. Remembering the end of our story, the true tale of the heavenly city we're headed for, empowers hope.

In this chapter, we will plan a worship festival, a time to share stories through a wide variety of media as part of the worship of a life of faith and hope. You will be called to step outside your comfort zone, perhaps, to write or create something that will stand to mark this season of growth. Get ready to burst into creativity for the sake of God's glory!

[Jesus] chose people who were still childlike enough to leave the known comforts of the daily world, the security of their jobs, their reasonable way of life, to follow him. . . . Unless we are creators, we are not fully alive.

—Madeleine L'Engle, *Walking on Water: Reflections on Faith and Art*

Story Feast Review

Review the instructions and ground rules for a story feast in chapter 3.

Plan Your Feasting Food

Feasts involve special foods. It may be a favorite treat you enjoy from the grocery store, or it could be your grandmother's banana pudding. What "ritual food" will you share at the feast? What significance does it have for you?

DAY 2

Plan Your Offering

1. Review the chapter titles, theological themes, and stories you told for each of the chapters. Make notes of any words or concepts that particularly capture your attention.

2. Here is a list of questions to consider about some of the major topics. Make a mark by any that you might like to work with for your project.

☐ "Faith is the assurance of things hoped for..." (Heb. 11:1 ESV).

What things are you hoping for? What things are you assured of?

☐ "Faith is... the conviction of things not seen" (Heb. 11:1 ESV).

What are the things not seen? What conviction do you have that these things will become a reality?

☐ They died without receiving the promises.

What promises has God made to us?

☐ Letting go...

What things might God be calling you to let go of or has he called you to let go of?

☐ "Looking forward..." (Heb. 11:10).

What things do you know about your calling? What more would you like to know?

☐ Celebrating surprise

Plan a surprise party to celebrate God's grace in your life.

☐ Laughter

Describe a time when God has invited you to laugh in a place of severe doubt.

☐ Suffering wait

Describe or depict a time of waiting in your life.

☐ Wrestling with redemption

When has God's redemption not fit your timing and your expectations?

☐ Rest

Return to your "Sabbath project" in the *Living Story* section of chapter 5. Describe how that Sabbath went, or try it again, adjusting in any way that you think would make it more restful.

DAY 3

Prepare Your Offering

1. Choose one of the topics above, or blend several for the story you want to tell.

2. Choose your medium. The possibilities are as endless as the various personalities of different group members. Try to choose a project that you can complete in the allotted time. Alternatively, you can bring the plans for a creation-in-work. Here are some ideas to get you started:

   a. Written media: story, poem, drama, psalm, prayer

   b. Visual media: drawing, painting, video, scrapbook, collage, visual journal

   c. Musical media: song, music, recording

3. On your mark, get set, create. Just do it, and don't worry about whether it's perfect. This is a worship festival, not a competition!

DAY 4

Note: Throughout the rest of the chapter, we will refer to the creative project as the *story*.

1. Reflect on the story. Consider any or all of the following questions:

    a. What does this story reveal about you or about others? What does it reflect about your style of relating to others?

    b. What does this story show about who God is and what he has done?

c. Is there anything about the story that makes you question the goodness of the heart of God? If so, take those questions to him in prayer. (Review Psalm 77 for an excellent example of a psalmist crying out to God in confusion over the events of his life and the resultant reaffirmation of his faith.)

d. What does the story reveal about sin? Grace? Redemption?

e. Take your story to Scripture. Is there a story in the Bible that reminds you of yours? A character? A psalm?

DAY 5

1. Edit the story.

   a. After reflecting on the questions above, make any adjustments you think necessary.

   b. Take out details that aren't essential to the key point of the story.

   c. Add in details that would make the story clearer.

PREPARE TO SHARE THE STORY

Each group member will be allotted about ten minutes for sharing a story and hearing thoughts of others. In the case of various media, it will be good to explain your work. As with a written story, you may want to write an outline of your main points.

2. What will be the best way to share your project with others? If it is a written story, would you like to read your story or tell it?

3. Will you need any special props or equipment to share your project? Make arrangements for those ahead of time.

However you share your creative project, make sure that you have key points outlined. You've got only ten minutes, so it's important to focus on the essentials. Practice sharing the story beforehand to see how long it takes.

ᏟINALLY, THE ᏟEAST

Ideally, you should feast for about two and a half hours:

- 30 minutes: Feast and fellowship.
- 10 minutes: Leader introduces story theme and prays.
- 90 minutes (maximum): Story sharing. Ten minutes per person, so if your group is larger than nine people, divide into two smaller groups.
- 15 minutes: Close with a time of prayer for one another's stories.

EPILOGUE

We have traveled far and well together on this journey of faith and hope. And yet, if we simply stop here, our journey may have been for naught. If we've learned anything, it's that the story learned must be lived. Take a moment to remember and to celebrate the contours of the terrain you have walked.

DAY 1

Flip back through the study. Find your memory verses.

1. Write them all here or perhaps in a separate place where you can revisit them often.

Little by little, one travels far.

—J. R. R. Tolkien, *The Lord of the Rings*

2. Are any stories in your life related to the verses? Write at least the title of each story, or the whole story if you have time.

DAY 2

Revise your story from the final story feast. Consider the process of telling the story.

1. What kinds of responses did the group give you about your story?

2. How did you feel as you told your story?

3. Did you notice anything new about your story through the telling or through a group member's response?

DAY 3 & DAY 4

Write down any specific prayers that you will pray for other group members based on the stories you heard.

DAY 5

Finish the story. Write down some reflections on what you have learned over the course of this study and how it affects the way you live and love in God's story of grace.

In the already/not-yet era between Christ's first coming and his second, we struggle daily with living in faith, hope, and love. In parts 1 and 2 of the Living Story series, we have walked together in learning and living God's story of grace. In part 3, *Loving God's Story of Grace*, we will learn about bearing this good news to a broken world desperate to know it.

As we part for now, I urge you to stay close to a community who will remind you of the gospel, encourage you to believe and hope, and call you to love. Thank you for joining me on this journey, and if you'd like to share your stories, please contact me at etstory@earthlink.net, on Facebook at "Living Story," or at www.livingstorygrace.com. I look forward to meeting again soon to walk together through *Loving God's Story of Grace*.

Elizabeth

WORKS CITED

Allender, Dan. *Sabbath*. The Ancient Practices. Nashville: Thomas Nelson, 2009.

————. *The Healing Path*. Colorado Springs: Navpress, 1997.

Alter, Robert. *Genesis*. New York: Norton & Co., 1996.

Augustine. *Confessions*. Trans. Henry Chadwick. Oxford: Oxford University Press, 2008.

Calvin, John. *New Testament Commentaries*. 12 vols. Grand Rapids: Eerdmans, 1994.

Card, Michael. "They Called Him Laughter." *An Invitation to Awe* (compact disc). Sparrow Records, 2011. Permission granted in personal correspondence with composer on October 18, 2011,

Carmichael, Amy. *God's Missionary*. Fort Wayne, PA: CLC Publications, 2010.

Dawn, Marva. *Keeping the Sabbath Wholly: Ceasing, Resting, Embracing, Feasting*. Montreal: Augsburg, 2008.

DeYoung, Kevin. *The Good News We Almost Forgot: Discovering the Gospel in a 16th Century Catechism*. Chicago: Moody, 2010.

Duguid, Iain. *Living in the Gap between Promise and Reality*. Phillipsburg, NJ: P&R Publishing, 1999.

Harper, Douglas. "eschaton. Dictionary.com. Online Etymology Dictionary." *Dictionary.com*. 1935. http://dictionary.reference.com/browse/eschaton.

Helprin, Mark. "Monday." In *Pacific and Other Stories*. New York: Penguin, 2004.

Hughes, Philip Edgcumbe. *A Commentary on the Epistle to the Hebrews*. Grand Rapids: Eerdmans, 1977.

Keller, Tim. *Genesis: What Were We Put in the World to Do?* New York: Redeemer, 2006.

Kidner, Derek. *Genesis*. Downers Grove, IL: Inter-Varsity Press, 1967.

L'Engle, Madeleine. *Walking on Water: Reflections on Faith and Art*. New York: North Point Press, 1995.

Manning, Margaret. "The Incongruity Theory of Faith." April 22, 2008. Ravi Zacharias International Ministries. http://www.rzim.org/resources/read/asliceofinfinity/todaysslice.aspx?aid=9969.

Meyers, Jan. *The Allure of Hope*. Colorado Springs: NavPress, 2001.

Mote, Edward. "My Hope Is Built on Nothing Less." In *Trinity Hymnal*, no. 521. Suwanee, GA: Great Commission Publications, 1990.

Packer, J. I. *Concise Theology*. Wheaton, IL: Tyndale, 1995.

Peterson, Eugene. *Conversations: The Message with Its Translator*. Colorado Springs: NavPress, 2007.

Remen, Rachel Naomi. *Kitchen-Table Wisdom*. New York: Penguin, 2006.

Shaw, Luci. *The Crime of Living Cautiously: Hearing God's Call to Adventure*. Downers Grove, IL: InterVarsity Press, 2005.

Smith, Scotty. *The Reign of Grace*. West Monroe, LA: Howard, 2003.

Spurgeon, Charles H. ""The Obedience of Faith." August 21, 1890. *The Spurgeon Archive*. http://www.spurgeon.org/sermons/2195.htm.

Taylor, Daniel. *Tell Me a Story: The Life-Shaping Power of Our Stories*. St. Paul, MN: Bog Walk Press, 2001.

Tolkien, J. R. R. *The Lord of the Rings*. New York: Mariner Books, 2005.

Tripp, Paul David. *Instruments in the Redeemer's Hands*. Phillipsburg, NJ: P&R Publishing, 2002.

Wright, N. T. *The Crown and the Fire*. Grand Rapids: Eerdmans, 1992..

Also in the Living Story series

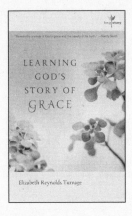

The grand narrative of Scripture sings a song of redemption in four parts: creation, the fall, redemption, and consummation. Woven through each part of the story is the unifying theme of *shalom*: peace, wholeness, and harmony. This great story tells how the peace of shalom began, how it was lost and hopelessly sought, how it was partially restored, and how it will one day be restored in full.

Scripture shows us that the smaller stories of our own lives matter, too. Our stories fit and find meaning in the Bible's grand story—and the narrative of shalom explains the loss, search, and future restoration of peace in our own lives.

In this meaningful, inviting, and encouraging study, Elizabeth Turnage lays out God's grand story and helps you see where your own story fits. Engaging questions allow you to apply not only the study, but also the entire story itself, to your own life. Unique sections help you engage Scripture and live out the gospel in your own story.

"Elizabeth draws me to understand God's story, my story, and Scripture like few others."

–Shari Thomas, Founding Director, Parakaleo

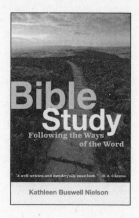
What is Bible study, anyway? The answers are many and diverse! Is it the same thing as just reading through the Bible, or does true Bible study involve treating the Bible differently from any other book?

Kathleen Nielson calls laypeople interested in Bible study to the crucial starting points and approaches that the Bible itself demands. She not only analyzes current trends, but also points the way forward.

Bible Study: Following the Ways of the Word winsomely highlights not a rigid set of methods, but a clear approach to Bible study—one that acknowledges the Scripture for what it is and faithfully enables us to take in the very words of God and submit ourselves to them. It examines just what Bible study should involve, according to the truths and principles given to us in the Bible itself.

"The book cannot be better than it is . . . it covers all the right topics in exactly the right order! For people who teach the Bible—or who aspire to teach it—this book will be the gold standard for knowing how to do it right."

—**Leland Ryken**, Professor of English, Wheaton College

More Bible Study resources from P&R Publishing

Susan Hunt guides women to explore prayers from the Bible, highlighting the overarching story of redemption that shapes these biblical prayers and equips us to know God's nearness and call on him in truth.

She passionately believes that only a true woman can do this—so she lays out foundational, biblical principles of true womanhood, showing that true women are redeemed women.

Prayers of the Bible is an excellent study for women's Bible study groups. Each prayer passage comes with an outline, questions to focus your thoughts, a prayer story, practical suggestions for prayer, and suggestions for personal reflection.

"Susan Hunt in this remarkable book gives a practical guide to the Christian who desires to bow lower and draw nearer to God in prayer."

–Joni Eareckson Tada, Joni and Friends International Disability Center

The Leader's Guide expands the material in *Prayers of the Bible* for small groups.